Mystical and Ethical Experience

Mystical and Ethical Experience

Gerry C. Heard

MERCER

ISBN 0-86554-149-3

All books published by Mercer University Press
are produced on acid-free paper that exceeds
the minimum standards set by the
National Historical Publications and Records Commission.

Library of Congress Cataloging in Publication Data
Heard, Gerry C. (Gerry Claud), 1945–
    Mystical and ethical experience.

    Bibliography: p. 79.
    Includes index.
    1. Mysticism.   2. Ethics.   3. Spiritual life.
    4. God—love.   5. Man (Theology)   I. Title.
    BL625.H35   1985   248.2'2   84-29569
    ISBN 0-86554-149-3

Contents

Foreword

In this book, Gerry C. Heard explores a variety of relationships between mystical and ethical experience. He advocates and defends the central claim that "a person can experience the Divine not only through the mystical but also through the ethical." He recognizes that his key terms may have a variety of meanings. For his purposes, he conceives of mystical experience broadly as that "in which God is experienced in a direct manner so that there is an immediate encounter with the Divine," and he develops the idea that this type of experience is dominated by "self-giving love." By contrast, ethical experience is defined as "encounter with God through our relationships in the universe." This is explicated to mean those relationships of duty to ourselves, other human beings, nonhuman life, and inanimate objects given to us in our basic ethical intuitions. Heard recognizes in his final chapter that the mystical and the ethical may exist and develop independently of one another, but he shows in some detail how persons are incomplete until the mystical and the ethical begin to exist in complementary relationships.

The central theme of this book is an important one for religious thought and serves as a significant corrective to one-sided views that emphasize religious belief, experience, or practice at the expense of the ethical, or vice versa. If Heard is correct in believing that the Divine is experienced both through and as ultimate mystical and ethical reality, then any complete experience of God or communication from God must make a place for both. It will include the ethical dimension of the Divine nature as well as the creative, redemptive, noetic, etc. Religious belief, experience and practice can never be isolated finally from social concern and moral action. Devotion to a God who is experienced as a loving God cannot be complete until it includes a devotion to all that God loves. Loving God fully inevitably involves loving neighbor as self, if God loves neighbor as self. Heard develops the theme that Jesus, whom he takes to be our model of God, lived out a social as well as a soteriological gospel.

Many readers will discover that Heard makes an important and innovative application of the principle of loving what God loves. He extends this principle to include loving and assuming moral responsibilities toward our nonhuman environment. Perhaps God also loves the world. He finds that this requires a development of more ethical relationships with animals and with all living and nonliving things than has been characteristic of us in the past.

The final outcome of Heard's book is a religious ethic very much akin to Jonathan Edwards's doctrine of "true virtue," which Edwards maintained "essentially consists in benevolence to Being in general. Or perhaps, to speak more accurately, it is that consent, propensity and union of heart to Being in general, that is immediately exercised in a general good will."[1]

The central message of Heard's book is simple but profound. The book is written clearly and the position is easy to understand with highly technical theological and philosophical jargon avoided. It is a good introduction to reflection on ethico-religious themes.

Rem B. Edwards
The University of Tennessee
Knoxville TN

---

[1]Jonathan Edwards, *The Nature of True Virtue* (Ann Arbor: The University of Michigan Press, 1960) 3.

Introduction

How does an individual experience God? A common understanding of an encounter with the Divine is that it is a mystical experience that is intuitive and often emotional in nature. Certainly this is one way of encountering the Divine, but is this the only way that man can experience God? Maybe there is some other means by which the Divine communicates with man. Perhaps God can also be known through others in what can be called ethical experiences.

A person can experience the Divine not only through the mystical but also through the ethical. That is, God can be experienced through our relationships with other beings in the universe as well as in a direct and intuitive manner. These descriptions of the mystical and the ethical, however, are highly general in character. What can be said more specifically about these categories? What exactly are the mystical and the ethical, and how are they related to each other?

This work sets forth and explicates the meaning and relationship of these two types of experiences of the Divine. These experiences, however, include both Divine and human elements; therefore, before investigating them in more detail, it is necessary to explain the nature of God and the human situation. Chapter one establishes that the basic and essential attribute of God is holy love, which includes the qualities of caring, empathy, and sharing. This love is revealed not only in the structure and operation of the universe, but also in the person of Jesus Christ. In chapter two it is demonstrated that the human situation is such that we are similar as well as dissimilar to other beings. We are like other beings in that we are interrelated with them and have a need to share ourselves with them, but we are different in that we are incomplete and free to decide whether we will accept the Divine nature.

Chapters three, four, and five are specifically concerned with explaining mystical and ethical experiences of the Divine and their relationship. Chapter three indicates that in a mystical experience God is known through a direct communication with him, a communication in which there is an immediate awareness of self-giving love by the individual. Chapter four points out that a person's ethical experiences represent his encounter with God through his relationships in the universe and that in these relationships an individual has responsibilities toward others and also himself. Chapter five shows that both the mystical and the ethical have the potential to help bring about the presence of the other type of experience and that in some cases mystical and ethical experiences interact with each other. It also reveals that the Divine is involved in the relationship between the mystical and the ethical and that an awareness of this relationship can enhance one's experiences of the Divine.

I

The Divine Nature

Our experiences of God are composed of the two fundamental elements of the Divine and the human. Each of these elements makes a significant contribution to the meaning of these experiences. Therefore, before giving attention to our specific encounters with God, first it is necessary to investigate both the Divine nature and the human situation. This beginning chapter examines the question of the nature of God and claims that this nature is basically and essentially one of self-giving love. This love includes the qualities of caring, empathy, and sharing and is revealed through the organization of the universe and the person of Jesus Christ.

The Divine Qualities

The Christian Scriptures and tradition point out numerous characteristics of God, and certainly the Divine possesses many qualities such as love, mercy, justice, and holiness, which are often spoken of and discussed. To accurately interpret the meaning of the Divine, however, it is necessary to focus on those qualities that are basic and essential to God's nature. That is, those qualities must be emphasized that enable us to explain other characteristics of the Divine and at the same time give us a correct and exact understanding of how God acts in the universe and in his contact with mankind. There are several criteria useful for determining these Divine qualities. One criterion is the attributes in the Christian Scriptures which get the most attention and are most strongly stressed. Another criterion is the explanatory power of the characteristic: which qualities through their overall meaning are able to explain a large number of other Divine qualities? A third criterion is our own relationship with the Divine: which characteristics are primary in God's revelation to man and our encounter with the Divine?

In using these criteria to appraise the various attributes of God, the general concept that emerges as basic and essential to the Divine nature is self-giving love. This love is God's willingness to reach out and give assistance to his creation. The Bible contains numerous references to this characteristic, and some of these directly point to God as being love or as practicing love.[1] There are many passages, however, that point to this Divine quality by emphasizing the need to carry out this love in our lives.[2] These passages serve as indirect references to God's loving nature in that we are being called upon to pattern our life after the Divine. Furthermore, this concept of self-giving love is basic for understanding other qualities of God. For example, Divine qualities such as mercy and justice are extensions of God's love. God carries out acts of mercy and justice because he cares for us and wants to help us be what we need to be. In addition, our encounter with God is for the most part an experience of this love. It is an experience of one who out of deep concern initiates a relationship with us in which he shows us the kind of life that is rewarding and fulfilling.

Along with this quality of self-giving love, the attribute of holiness also emerges as being basic and essential to the Divine nature. This quality points to the uniqueness of the Divine nature by referring to God as being without sin and as being set apart from that which is finite. God's holiness is highly emphasized in the Scriptures,[3] and it also has strong explanatory power in the sense that other Divine qualities can be viewed as being in-

---

[1]See John 3:16, II Corinthians 13:11, and I John 4:16.

[2]See Matthew 22:37-39, John 13:34-35, and Romans 13:8.

[3]See Psalms 89:35, Isaiah 5:16, and Revelation 4:8.

cluded within God's distinctive nature. Moreover, our experience of the Divine easily elicits a response of awe and reverence because it is an encounter with the Holy One.

The Divine characteristics of holiness and love are not rival concepts, but are complementary in that Divine love gives content to the concept of holiness. God is pure self-giving love, which sets him apart from the nature of man. Certainly there are other qualities that contribute to God's uniqueness, but God's revelation shows us that self-giving love must be regarded as the most important of these qualities. That is, God has demonstrated to us through Scripture and our experiences of him that this love is the primary means by which he is to be understood.

The recognition of the significance of Divine love for comprehending God's holiness is found to some degree in the prophets of the Old Testament. They protested against the acceptance of merely a ceremonial holiness in which the Holy One is identified with religious ritual at the neglect of ethical behavior. They had begun to realize that the Holy One is a God of love and that he demands righteous conduct from his people. It is in the revelation through Jesus Christ that this holy love is more clearly presented. Jesus got involved in the lives of those around him and ministered to their needs. He exemplified Divine love in his interaction with others. He did this because he realized that God is distinctive in the sense of being self-giving love and not in the sense of being separated from the human situation.

It is holy love that is the basic and essential characteristic of the Divine. Up to this point this concept has only been presented in highly general terms. What exactly is the meaning of this concept? What is the nature of Divine love? One way of answering this question is to carefully examine God's involvement in the universe. The revelation of God in the universe demonstrates the various qualities of Divine love.

God in the Universe

In observing the work of the Divine within the universe, it first is noticeable that God's love includes the qualities of care and empathy. Regarding care, Rollo May says that it ". . . is a state in which something does matter; care is the opposite of apathy."[4] "It means to wish someone

---

[4]Rollo May, *Love and Will* (New York: Dell Publishing Co., Inc., 1969) 286.

well. . . ."[5] This state of caring is a vital part of God's attitude toward the universe. His presence in every phase of nature, both the organic and the inorganic, indicates the care that he has for it. He considers the universe to be valuable, and he is interested in it. At the same time, he wants the best for it. He wants it to be what he knows it should be, and he actively seeks to encourage it in that direction.

God's care for the universe provides the basis for his willingness to act on its behalf. Furthermore, his empathy is the foundation for his ability to share with the universe what it needs. God is able to provide the proper assistance for the universe because he possesses empathy. May explains the derivation of the word "empathy."

> Empathy comes to us as a translation of the word of the German psychologists, "einfuhlung" which means literally "feeling into." It is derived from the Greek "pathos," meaning a deep and strong feeling akin to suffering, prefixed with the preposition "in."[6]

Empathy is the ability to identify with another so fully that there is a participation in the other's being. One assumes the state of the other so that one is able to feel, think, or just exist as the other does. At the same time, the one that is exercising empathy gives up awareness of himself. His attention is directed toward the other, causing him to forget about himself. In order to demonstrate the meaning of empathy, May gives the example of artistic experience.

> In artistic experience empathy is also basic, for the individual must in some way identify himself with the object if he is to experience it aesthetically. Thus people speak of music "carrying them away," or of the violin playing upon the strings of their emotions, or of the changing colors of the sunset creating a corresponding change in their emotions. . . . Drama is the form of art in which empathy is most easily understood, for there occurs the very obvious identification of the actors with the fictitious characters they are representing, as well as the more subtle identification of the observers with the actors.[7]

---

[5]Ibid., 389.

[6]Rollo May, *The Art of Counseling* (Nashville: Abingdon Press, 1939) 75.

[7]Ibid., 78.

The goal of empathy is not determined by empathy itself, but by the one who is practicing it. Empathy may serve as a basis for acts of love, but it may also be used simply as a means of attaining pleasure or knowledge. In the case of Divine empathy, the ultimate goal is always to share for the good of the other. God wants to provide for the needs of the universe, and empathy aids him in implementing this purpose.

Through his empathy God participates in the being of the particulars of the universe, and in this way he is able to know their individual conditions. This is true of his love for both the animate and inanimate objects of existence. God is conscious of the situation of various plants and animals, but he is also aware of the status of inorganic substances such as air, water, and soil. Divine empathy is directed not only toward particular beings, but toward the universe as a whole. As a result of his identification with the whole, God understands the interrelationships between the parts of the universe. He is cognizant, for example, of the effect that mankind has had upon other animals and upon the air and water of the planet.

Through empathy God gains an awareness of the state of the universe and its constituents. This knowledge is a necessary foundation for his being able to give assistance to the universe. It enables him to extend to others what they need for their advancement. This points to another quality of Divine love—the act of sharing. God not only cares for the universe and empathizes with it, but he is willing to act on its behalf and share himself with it.

The universe itself points to this sharing nature of the Divine. It shows that God has shared himself with it in that he has provided the universe with what he is; that is, he has given the universe some of the traits that he possesses. An example of these qualities is orderliness. God is orderly because there is harmony within his being. The various characteristics of his existence work together rather than in opposition to each other. God's wrath, for instance, is not in contradiction to his love, but rather it is a way that his love is expressed. At times God's love takes the form of wrath in order to discipline and correct those who go against his will. In addition, the harmony of the Divine nature is also presented through the consistency of his acts. None of his acts violate any of his previous acts, and each points to the kind of being that he is.

This Divine harmony is reflected in the universe that God has cre-ated. One way that this occurs is through the organization of our solar sys-tem. For example, the distance of the earth from the sun makes it possible for life to exist. Also, the rotation of the earth on its axis provides periods of light and dark as well as periods of warmth and cooling, and the revo-lutions of the earth around the sun make possible the different seasons of the year. Aspects of our solar system such as these point to the orderly way in which the universe operates.

This orderliness is also present through the interrelationships of the different parts of the earth and its environment. Our planet's system con-sists of a variety of forms, both inorganic and organic, which are interre-lated in such a fashion so as to provide for their continued existence. This interrelation is revealed first of all in the dependence of the organic realm upon the inorganic. Inorganic matter provides the environment for the organic phase of nature in that life is located in and upon the inanimate, and the nonliving substances provide the necessary elements for life to ex-ist. Plants need soil, air, sunlight, and water, and animals rely upon air, water, and heat. Furthermore, there is an interdependence between plants and animals, such as in the carbon dioxide-oxygen life cycle. Plants are in need of the carbon dioxide exhaled by animals, and animals must have the oxygen that is given off by plants. Animals also need the nour-ishment that comes from particular types of plants. All forms of animal life, including man, receive their sustenance either entirely from plants themselves, from other animals that consume plants, or through both of these means. In addition, there is interdependence both among plants and within the animal kingdom. Plants as well as animals rely upon the previous reproductive activities of their own kind in order to come into being, and animals need the care and protection of other animals during the early stages of development.

God has given the universe some of what he is himself by providing it with an orderly structure. Orderliness, however, is not the only quality God has provided for the universe. It is interesting to note that he has given it a sharing nature. This vital part of God's existence is also found in the universe as the necessary nature of relationships. A being must share himself with others before he can truly be himself. This means that God has not merely provided an orderly universe in which a variety of things are able to continue existing. He simultaneously has made it possible for these forms of being to practice self-giving and thereby to have a rewarding existence in relation to each other.

This activity of sharing is constantly taking place in the universe as both organic and inorganic beings make contributions to the existence of other beings: the practice of adult organisms protecting and training their young, dead organisms providing food for other organisms and fertilizer for the soil, and air and water contributing to the lives of plants and animals. These examples indicate that the various beings of the universe share their capacities with others and even at times sacrifice themselves so others might exist.

Thus, an examination of the universe and God's relationship to it indicates that Divine love consists of the qualities of caring, empathy, and sharing. Moreover, another way that the meaning of this love has been manifested is through the lives of other people. Perhaps everyone at some time during his life has demonstrated one of these Divine qualities, at least to a minor degree. No doubt there have been certain individuals through whom these qualities have been revealed in a more extensive manner. In particular, one person, Jesus Christ, serves as the highest example of the manifestation of the Divine nature through the human. It was in him that God gave a complete revelation of himself.

God in Jesus Christ

Each of the qualities of Divine love is fully presented through the person of Jesus Christ. For instance, the importance of caring is included in the teachings of Jesus. He taught that there should be no limit to our attitude of goodness toward others. It should be directed toward everyone regardless of whether there is love in return, and it should even be extended to one's enemies.[8] Jesus demonstrated this quality in his relationships with others. He did not let the standards of his society restrict the amount of concern that he showed toward other people. He often opposed the expectations of the majority and expressed interest in people that most of society either rejected or ignored, such as the sick, afflicted, poor, unattractive, and those considered unworthy by society. Although Jesus was frequently criticized for the concern that he showed for these people, he was willing to associate with them and seek to minister to their needs.

---

[8]Matthew 5:43-48.

In fact, he said it was their needs that led him to associate with them. On one occasion the Pharisees were being critical of Jesus for dining with a group of tax collectors and with others who were thought of as sinners by most of society. When questioned as to why he was eating with these people, his response was that those in need of assistance are the sick, not those who are healthy.[9]

Blindness was prevalent in the first century, and no doubt many people in Palestine took it for granted and simply ignored those so stricken. Jesus, however, showed an interest in the blind. There are several references in the New Testament to this.[10] In one instance a blind beggar named Bartimaeus was sitting by the road as Jesus and others were leaving Jericho. Bartimaeus was crying out repeatedly for Jesus to show him mercy. Many of the people who were gathered there obviously wanted to ignore his cries, for they told him to be quiet, but Jesus made an effort to talk with Bartimaeus and was able to restore his sight.[11]

Another example of Jesus' caring attitude was the relationship that he had with Zacchaeus. Zacchaeus was a wealthy tax collector in Jericho. He probably was extremely alienated from others and lonely, for tax collectors generally were unpopular because of forceful and unethical tactics used in collecting taxes. Jesus cared for Zacchaeus in spite of who he was and in spite of the prejudices of the people. He was willing to visit and talk with him in his home. This was a radical act for a man of Jesus' reputation to be associating with a tax collector, but Jesus was willing to do it because of his deep compassion. As a result of the contact that Jesus had with Zacchaeus, Zacchaeus was able to acquire a new outlook on life. Zacchaeus proclaimed that he would give half his possessions to the poor, and if he had cheated anyone, he would repay that person four times the amount he had taken.[12]

This incident points to the empathy that Jesus possessed in his relationships with others. He was able to identify with the circumstances of both Zacchaeus and the crowd. Consequently, he understood that Zacchaeus felt separated from others and that he needed to be accepted and

---

[9]Matthew 9:10-13.

[10]See Matthew 9:27-31, Mark 8:22-26, and John 9:1-41.

[11]Mark 10:46-52.

[12]Luke 19:1-10.

treated with kindness. He was aware of the people's animosity toward Zacchaeus; therefore, he knew that they needed to be shown that they were wrong in their treatment of Zacchaeus and that regardless of his acts as a tax collector, he still deserved to be given consideration.

Jesus was capable of going beyond the common human characteristic of predominantly directing one's concentration and concern toward oneself. He could get outside of himself in the sense of being able to put aside his own interests and desires. As a result, he was capable of participating in the inward self of another. He could take on their state of existence and experience their motives, feelings, and thoughts. This gave him understanding about the situations of others and their needs.

Another example of Jesus' empathy was the incident with Mary of Bethany. On this occasion, Jesus was being given a supper in his honor, and Mary brought a pound of expensive perfume and used it to anoint the feet of Jesus. Judas Iscariot was critical of Mary's act, insisting that this perfume should have been sold and the money given to the poor. However, Jesus empathized with both Mary and Judas, understanding both their motives. He knew that Mary's act was one of appreciation and love for him. At the same time, he realized that Judas was not really interested in the poor, but simply wanted to get the money for himself. As treasurer of the group, Judas knew that the money would be turned over to him, thus giving him the opportunity to seize some of it for himself.[13]

Both care and empathy were present in the life of Jesus. Yet, care and empathy alone are not sufficient to describe Jesus' love for others, for he did not think of love as being only a motive or inward feeling. Through his teachings and life-style, he demonstrated that love is active. It involves acts of sharing oneself with others. Jesus pointed out in his teachings the need to share. On one occasion a wealthy man of the ruling class asked Jesus what he should do to gain eternal life. Jesus told him it was not enough merely to obey the commandments. He should sell everything he had and distribute the money to the poor. In other words, Jesus was calling on the man to share what he had with others. One must not only avoid directly harming others, but be willing to sacrifice and practice giving toward others.[14]

---

[13]John 12:1-8.

[14]Luke 18:18-27.

Jesus told a lawyer the story of the good Samaritan to illustrate that the true neighbor is the one who shares himself. In the story the Levite and the priest saw the injured man on the roadside, and to some degree they may have cared for the man and empathized with him, but they were not willing to share themselves with the man by offering help. It was the Samaritan who did this. He shared his time by stopping, he shared his talents by treating and bandaging the man's wounds, he shared his beast to carry the man to the inn, and he shared his money so that the man could be provided for by the innkeeper. Not only was the Samaritan sympathetic toward the injured man, but he was willing to get involved in the man's situation in an active way. [15]

Jesus did not simply tell others about the importance of sharing. He also shared himself in numerous ways through his contact with others. He shared his time and efforts with his disciples by training and teaching them. He healed the sick and afflicted and ministered to the outcasts of society, such as the poverty-stricken and those that were labeled sinners. Moreover, he shared himself in the ultimate sense in that he died for the sins of mankind. He gave himself as a sacrifice so that others might be rejoined with God. Hence, like the structure and function of the universe, the life and death of Jesus Christ also indicates that Divine love includes the attributes of caring, empathy, and sharing. Through Jesus Christ these qualities were given a human expression. They were presented through human motives and actions as Jesus interacted with the people of his time. Therefore, Jesus shows us what God is like as a human being. He serves as a personal model for us to relate to.

Yet, Jesus Christ is the agent of the redemptive process for mankind and not just a model of the Divine nature. That is, God has given us Jesus Christ to show us the Divine nature and in turn what he wants us to be but no individual besides Jesus fully obeys the Divine nature and completely carries out a life of caring, empathy, and sharing. Instead, each person goes against the Divine nature or, in other words, sins against God. [16] This breaks the relationship between the individual and God, and because sin is continually present in every life, the relationship with the Divine cannot be reestablished through human efforts. Out of his love for

---

[15] Luke 10:25-37.

[16] Romans 3:23.

man, however, God sets up a means whereby it is possible for an individual to be rejoined with him through the redemptive act of Jesus Christ.

This redemptive act is Jesus' identification with the sins of mankind and his willingness to die to overcome these sins. The care that Jesus had for others led him to empathize with all human beings. Through his empathy, he put himself in the place of others and took upon himself their condition. He so completely empathized with others that he acquired their sin. In this sense he became sin for the sake of others.[17] In addition, he was willing to share himself in a way that would enable this sin to be overcome. That is, he was willing to die for the sake of others, and it was through his death that sin was defeated. This means that a person can be reunited with the Divine through the assistance of Jesus Christ. A new relationship with God is now possible through Jesus Christ, but this new relationship is not automatic. It requires an individual to renounce the life-style that opposes the Divine nature and to accept the Spirit of Christ into his inward self.

To summarize, the basic and essential quality of God is holy love. It is this love that enables us to explain other characteristics of the Divine and gives us an accurate understanding of the way God acts in the universe and in relation to man. Furthermore, the structure and operation of the universe and the person of Jesus Christ reveal that the nature of this love is one of caring, empathy, and sharing. God cares for his creation, empathizes with it, and is willing to share himself with it.

This completes the investigation of the Divine nature, which is one of the basic elements in the experience of God. The other major element, the human component, must also be explored before discussing the different types of encounters with the Divine. It is necessary, therefore, to turn now to an examination of the meaning of the human situation.

---

[17]II Corinthians 5:21.

Gerry C. Heard

Discussion Questions

1. Do you agree that holy love is the basis and essential characteristic of the Divine? How would you explain the relationship between God's love and God's wrath?

2. What is the difference between ceremonial holiness and ethical holiness? What effect might the acceptance of ceremonial holiness as the only form of holiness have upon a person's life?

3. What are the various ways that people use empathy in our society? Can empathy be used to attain any other goals besides pleasure, knowledge, and acts of love?

4. What examples are given in the chapter to demonstrate the sharing nature of the universe? What are some other examples that could be mentioned?

5. What individuals in the history of mankind would you say have revealed the Divine nature in an extensive way? Do you know any persons today who especially reveal the Divine nature?

6. Are there groups in our society today that we tend to ignore or avoid because they are unattractive or considered unworthy? If so, which groups would you mention?

7. What does Jesus' frequent association with the outcasts of society have to say about the nature of Christian ministry today?

8. Why is it often so difficult to make the transition from being caring and empathic to carrying out acts of sharing? What obstacles would you mention that sometimes serve to prevent us from making this transition?

9. What is meant by the redemptive act of Jesus Christ? Is this act completely finished, or is there a sense in which the Spirit of Christ continues this redemptive act today?

Suggestions for Further Reading

Aulen, Gustaf. *Christus Victor*. New York: Macmillan Publishing Co., Inc., 1969.

——————. *The Faith of the Christian Church*. Philadelphia: Fortress Press, 1960.

Baillee, D. M. *God Was in Christ*. New York: Charles Scribner's Sons, 1948.

Cobb, John B., and Griffin, David Ray. *Process Theology: An Introductory Exposition*. Philadelphia: The Westminster Press, 1976.

Fromm, Erich. *The Art of Loving*. New York: Harper and Row, Publishers, Inc., 1956.

Gaylin, Willard. *Caring*. New York: Alfred A. Knopf, Inc., 1976.

Hick, John. *The Center of Christianity*. San Francisco: Harper and Row, Publishers, Inc., 1968.

——————. *God Has Many Names*. Philadelphia: The Westminster Press, 1980.

Humphreys, Fisher. *Thinking about God: An Introduction to Christian Theology*. New Orleans: Insight Press Inc., 1974.

Manson, T. W. *The Teaching of Jesus*. Cambridge: Cambridge University Press, 1967.

May, Rollo. *The Art of Counseling*. Nashville: Abingdon Press, 1939.

——————. *Love and Will*. New York: Dell Publishing Co., Inc., 1969.

Phillips, J. B. *Your God Is Too Small*. New York: The Macmillan Company, 1961.

Roark, Dallas M. *The Christian Faith*. Nashville: Broadman Press, 1969.

Robinson, John A. T. *Honest to God*. Philadelphia: The Westminster Press, 1963.

Stewart, James S. *The Life and Teaching of Jesus Christ*. New York: Abingdon Press, n.d.

Whitehead, Alfred North. *Process and Reality*. New York: Harper and Row, Publishers, Inc., 1929.

——————. *Religion in the Making*. Cleveland: The World Publishing Company, 1926.

Williams, Daniel Day. *The Spirit and the Forms of Love*. New York: Harper and Row, Publishers, Inc., 1968.

II

The Human Situation

    This chapter focuses upon the human element in our experiences of God and explains the nature of our relationship to other beings and to the Divine. It points out that there is both a basic affinity and a basic difference between ourselves and other beings. We are like other beings in that we are part of an interdependent system and have a need to share ourselves with others, but we are distinct from others in the sense that we are incomplete and free to decide whether we will adopt the Divine nature. This chapter contends that the human situation is such that we tend to be guided by our narrow self-interests; therefore, we have a need to carry out acts of self-denial so that the Divine may more extensively become a part of our lives.

Our Affinity with Other Beings

    As indicated in chapter one, the universe is an interrelated system with its various types of existing things dependent upon each other. Human beings are part of this system and are dependent upon not only other life forms, but also the inanimate realm of existence. Plants and animals provide us with the basic items of food, shelter, and clothing, but these are not the only ways that we benefit from other living things. There is the beauty of plants and animals, which we are able to enjoy, along with the companionship that they offer. It is also true that mankind has gained a great deal in terms of understanding the human body and overcoming diseases and afflictions as a result of studying these other kinds of life. In addition, the inanimate phase of nature contributes to human life in various ways. Just as we could not exist without nonhuman life, we could not live without this realm. It provides us with such necessities as air, water, and heat, and it enables us to have further experiences of beauty through, for example, the presence of a waterfall or sunset. Still other contributions made to our life by inorganic nature include substances used in medicine, constituents for shelter, instruments, and machinery, and sources of energy.

Not only are we dependent upon other beings, but there is an important sense in which they are dependent upon us. Human beings have capacities such as memory, conceptualization, reason, imagination, and language, which are either not present at all in other beings or not present to as great a degree. These capacities enable us to have a significant amount of influence upon the way in which other things exist and interact with each other. Humans are powerful beings because we have the ability to change the course of nature. On the one hand, we can protect and enhance the existence of other beings, but on the other hand, it is possible for us to harm and even destroy them. We are able, for instance, to remove animals from a particular environment to protect them from extinction or from a natural disaster such as a flood; yet we are capable of destroying the animal life in a given environment and even causing the extinction of certain species through apathy, ignorance, laziness or greed.

As part of the interdependent system of nature, we are like other beings. We are dependent upon others, and they are dependent upon us. There is another fundamental similarity between ourselves and other types of beings. As already pointed out, other beings in the universe share themselves in numerous ways, but it is the case that we have a sharing responsibility in nature. God has given humanity the special role of being the manager of his creation. We oversee the various activities of the universe and make decisions about whether or not to make alterations in nature. At the same time, God has provided us with certain advanced capacities that aid us in our managerial task. These abilities as well as our position of manager serve to set us apart from everything else. These traits, however, must not be interpreted simply as a means of being distinct from others. We must view them as an indication of our similarity to others. We must understand that just as other beings have ways of sharing themselves, this is a means that we have of sharing.

In order to properly carry out this sharing responsibility, it is necessary for us to cooperate with God's activities and seek to assist him in his work in the universe. This means that we must remain in close relationship to God and strive to be an expression of self-giving love for all the beings in nature. This in turn demands that we place a high value upon all existence. All beings must be afforded intrinsic value and not merely instrumental value. That is, all existing things must be perceived as having value in themselves and not just value as a means to something else. Therefore, nonhuman life and nonliving phenomena are not simply to be looked upon as something that serves or gratifies man in some way. The value of these other beings is not entirely determined by the contribution that they make to human life, but instead they have a certain worth simply because they are existing beings. We must appreciate the various roles of the other beings of the universe and respect their right to exist and function as they do. This would preclude the unnecessary exploitation and waste of both the organic and inorganic environment. It would oppose, for example, the selfish mistreatment of animals, as well as the mass dumping of wastes into our waters, and the widespread pollution of the air with toxic gases.

Our Distinction from Other Beings

As part of an interdependent system, human beings need to share themselves with others, as do other beings of the universe. There is, however, a significant difference between humans and other beings. Jean-Paul Sartre illustrates this difference through his claim that the being of those existents, which are not self-conscious, perfectly coincides with itself. This means that their being is complete in itself so that they are wholly determined by whatever they are. Consequently, there is no possibility of their becoming other than what they are—they simply are what they are. In contrast, self-conscious being has nothingness at its center. Nothingness necessarily accompanies human reality, and it is this nothingness or lack of being that prevents the self from being able to coincide with himself. That is, nothingness is that which separates us from being something definite and complete. In being aware of our nothingness, however, we are able to conceive of what in actuality we are not. We understand that we are not all we can be, but at the same time we want to be more than what we actually are. Through our choices we are constantly seeking to overcome this lack in our being. Although we can never entirely rid ourselves of this nothingness, we are free to pursue those possibilities that we want to make a part of ourselves.[1] At one point Sartre summarizes the human condition in the following manner:

> Human reality is not something which exists first in order afterwards to lack this or that; it exists first as lack and in immediate, synthetic connection with what it lacks. Thus the pure event by which human reality rises as a presence in the world is apprehended by itself as its own lack. In its coming into existence human reality grasps itself as an incomplete being. It apprehends itself as being insofar as it is not, in the presence of the particular totality which it lacks and which it is in the form of not being it and which is what it is. Human reality is a perpetual surpassing toward a coincidence with itself which is never given.[2]

As Sartre says, the elements of incompleteness and freedom are characteristics of human beings only. As a result, other members of the universe must follow their own particular expression of sacrifice and sharing. Inorganic matter must be what its constitution dictates, and lower forms of life are directed by their inner functions and instincts. In contrast, however, human existence is not so highly determined. We are free to examine ourselves and our surroundings and to choose in what way we want to act in relation to others. We are confronted by various factors from our environment and our biological and psychological makeup, yet we still to some degree have the opportunity of choosing the manner in which we will respond to these factors.

The choices that we make arise out of an opposition within our being. We must choose in the midst of opposition, for at the same time that we are a being of possibilities, we are also a being of conflict between our need to be like the Divine and our tendency to let our selfish desires control our

---

[1]Jean-Paul Sartre, *Being and Nothingness* (New York: Washington Square Press, Inc., 1953) lxxiv-lxxx, 26-55, 89-103, 108-25, 208-27, 589-99.

[2]Ibid., 109.

actions. Each person has the potential for making choices that grow out of a loving attitude, but we are held back by narrow self-interests.

The Christian Scriptures use the term "sin" to refer to this element of self-centeredness within us that interferes with the Divine. Briefly stated, it is that which separates us from what we ought to be. As Paul Tillich says:

> We know that we are estranged from something to which we really belong, and with which we should be united. . . . It is this which is the state of our entire existence, from its very beginning to its very end. . . . It is our existence itself. Existence is separation![3]

According to Tillich, each person to some extent is always alienated from God, himself, and others. It is a state of human existence, but at the same time, it is something that we choose to make a part of ourselves. Each of us inevitably chooses an alienated existence. This alienation consists of both unbelief and self-elevation. Unbelief is our turning away from the Divine as the center of our lives; it is our will being separated from the Divine. Self-elevation is our turning toward ourselves as the center of the world. Included in this self-elevation is an unwillingness on our part to acknowledge the limitations of our being such as ignorance, insecurity, loneliness, and anxiety.[4]

Each of us to some degree does exist in a state of estrangement, as Tillich says, because the qualities of caring, empathy, and sharing are never fully present in our lives. To some extent we are always rejecting the Divine and accepting an outlook of distorted self-love. We are constantly letting self-interest play a part in our being, which lessens our caring, empathic, and sharing attitude toward others. That is, each individual is always overemphasizing his own desires so that he is never completely able to love other beings in the universe. This results in each person's separation to some extent from himself and from others. We cannot be what we need to be, and at best our relationships with others only approximate genuineness. Our experiences of fulfillment are, therefore, modified from

---

[3]Paul Tillich, *The Shaking of the Foundations* (New York: Charles Scribner's Sons, 1948) 155.

[4]Ibid., 154-55; Paul Tillich, *Systematic Theology* (Chicago: The University of Chicago Press, 1957) 2:44-58.

the ideal, thus we are unable to experience the unqualified joy from being a pure expression of the Divine.

Our estrangement is at its basis an alienation from the Divine. We can never completely express the Divine nature and, consequently, can never fulfill ourselves in the ultimate sense in our relationships. Even though we cannot reach the ideal, we are capable of more extensively incorporating the Divine into our being, thereby reducing the influence that this estrangement has upon our life. This demands that we renounce our narrow self-interests and accept the Spirit of Christ into our inward self. Of course, this acceptance does not imply that the individual becomes identical with the Divine and is able to carry out the Divine qualities in the same way that Jesus Christ practiced them. Sin always affects our human condition, at least in this life. This acceptance of Jesus Christ implies a closer relationship with the Divine. It implies that the Divine nature has a greater influence upon the individual, both in his understanding of himself and in his interaction with others.

Our Need for Self-Denial

Before the Spirit of Christ can be acquired, there must be a renunciation of self-centeredness by the individual. This renunciation is basic to a more thorough incorporation of the Divine. Jesus emphasized this need for self-denial in his teachings and spoke of it as being necessary for discipleship. He pointed out that we must put aside our preoccupation with ourselves in order to follow him.[5] Self-denial is not simply a single act that only needs to be accepted and carried out on one occasion. Instead, it is something that must be sustained through a sequence of acts. In other words, renunciation of narrow self-interests has to be constantly reaffirmed and practiced. The individual must be willing to practice acts of self-denial on numerous occasions and under a variety of circumstances.

When self-denial takes place, the individual is able to transcend his own private situation in order to assist in the needs of another. For example, a salesperson may think predominantely in terms of simply persuading a potential buyer to purchase a product and simultaneously have little regard for whether the item is actually needed or even wanted by the customer. In this situation, if estrangement is to be overcome and a caring

---

[5]Matthew 16:24-25, Mark 8:34-35, and Luke 9:23-24.

attitude allowed to operate, it is necessary that the salesperson to some extent practice a denial of his or her own narrow concerns. This enables the salesperson to render a higher level of service to the customer.

Not all acts that overtly appear to be expressions of self-renunciation actually are such in the true sense. For instance, there are situations in which individuals are willing to give their services or money to a charity or organization as long as they receive recognition in return. If this recognition is not provided, then these individuals will not make a contribution. In such cases as these, there is the willingness to practice some degree of self-denial as long as the results include some personal reward. In this type of self-denial, according to Søren Kierkegaard,

> Men will sacrifice this or that and everything, but they still hope to be understood and thereby to remain in a meaningful human context in which one's sacrifices are recognized and rejoiced over. They will leave everything, but they do not mean thereby to be deprived of the good opinion and understanding of men.[6]

In contrast, in true self-renunciation the actions of individuals are not motivated by self-interests, but by the desire to give assistance to others. In such cases, these individuals do not expect any reward for their actions, which reflects their willingness to deny themselves in situations in which there is no possibility of receiving praise, favor, or money from others. In fact, there is a willingness to renounce their own interests even though they are hated for their actions. In other words, self-denial is practiced even when criticism or ridicule is experienced in return.[7]

Although self-denial usually is discussed in terms of an individual's relationships with other people, it has reference to all of our relationships in the universe. It needs to be extended not only toward other people, but toward other types of beings. There are many examples of possible acts of self-denial in these other areas. There is the need for individuals and firms who raise animals for human consumption to improve the crowded conditions under which these animals are raised and transported. In the organic realm, certain plant life, such as the redwood trees of California, need protection from being destroyed for commercial purposes. In the in-

---

[6]Søren Kierkegaard, *Works of Love* (New York: Harper and Row, 1962) 133.

[7]Ibid., 133-34, 188-90, 336-43.

organic realm, there exists the need for some cities to improve their gar-
bage and sewage disposal. Such acts as these would improve our
relationships with other beings, but at the same time they demand that
we be willing to relinquish some personal conveniences as well as make
certain financial sacrifices.

Our acts of self-renunciation must give consideration to the whole of
nature. As our society has become aware of the adverse effects of pollution
upon the human species, an emphasis upon protecting the environment
has emerged. The thrust of this emphasis, however, has often been that
we must protect ourselves. It is pointed out that our existence is inextric-
ably connected with the rest of existence, and if we do not control pollution, it is inevitable that we will suffer serious harm. There is no doubt
that this emphasis carries with it considerable force. We do need to protect our environment to assure our own well-being, but should our betterment and survival be the only concern of environmental protection? If
other beings besides us are thought to have value in themselves, this
means that the maintenance of the environment should be not only for
our own sake, but for the benefit of other existing things as well. Our actions to overcome the exploitation of nature and to improve particular environmental situations should be aimed at aiding every being in the
universe, not just human beings.

In some cases individuals are willing to sacrifice their immediate personal interests in order to aid all of mankind. For example, an individual
or group may practice a type of self-denial in relation to nature, even
though they may be thinking exclusively in terms of man's benefit. For
instance, a group may cease dumping its wastes into a nearby river, not
just to protect itself, but to protect the rest of mankind as well. Acts of
this kind certainly have merit, since they avoid the level of narrow personal interests and also have beneficial consequences for nature. They are
not, however, expressions of self-renunciation in its fullest sense. They
reject the narrow concerns of a part of humanity, but in motivation, at
least, they do not transcend the restricted interests of humanity. They remain within the limited perspective of one kind of being and do not make
an effort to encompass the whole of nature.

The Divine Persuasion

Self-denial has application to our relationships with all types of beings
and should be utilized with a concern for the welfare of every realm of na-

ture. Even though this practice needs to be carried out by each individual, this does not imply that it is merely a result of human initiative. God is also involved in this process because of his care for man. He identifies with man's predicament through his empathic nature, and he gives man assistance in overcoming his alienation. He shares himself with mankind by providing encouragement for each person to practice self-renunciation and to adopt the Divine attitude. God's encouragement toward self-denial and toward himself is the work of the Divine persuasion within the human situation. God is always seeking to lead each individual to realize the importance of relinquishing narrow self-interests and accepting self-giving love. He wants each person to develop a caring and empathizing approach toward all beings so that every person will be able to share himself with the other members of the universe.

God uses various means to persuade us toward his nature. One of these is the assistance of certain human feelings. A person's concentration upon his own narrow interests may bring about disturbing and painful feelings such as despair and loneliness. These feelings can stimulate the individual toward reflection and an alteration in his outlook. In addition, acts of self-giving often result in sensations such as joy and fulfillment, which allow the individual to appreciate himself and to feel a sense of belonging with the universe. Consequently, when an individual experiences these positive feelings and realizes that they accompany a self-giving attitude, he often wishes to continue in this approach to life in the future.

Another means that God uses to persuade us toward him is the activity of human thought. On some occasions God is able to work through the interaction of our thinking and the power of truth to encourage us to alter our approach to life in some manner. For instance, we may be introduced to an idea such as one claiming that each of us has a duty to make sacrifices in order to help starving and diseased people in the world. God may work through the presentation of an idea such as this, and we may become convinced of its truth and possibly even be willing to perform acts of benevolence that we once rejected. This kind of example indicates that God may work in human thought through an idea that is set forth by someone else, but it is also possible for God to work through those situations that are primarily centered in our own examination of ourselves. There are times in which we reflect on our ideas and question their truth. Of course, these doubts do not in themselves mean that the idea is in error in some way. We should be aware, however, that God does sometimes work through the doubting process. He uses this process at times to encourage us to go beyond false concepts and partial truths and to expand our knowledge of his nature and what we should be.

The Divine persuasion also operates through the experience of certain events. An individual may have an experience that changes his attitude and life-style and helps him develop to some degree an acceptance of Divine love. For example, the occurrence of diseases and accidents may cause a person to reflect upon his life and in some cases to adopt a more honest understanding of himself and his relationships to others. God does not merely seek to encourage individuals toward himself through the occurrence of events that are in some respects unpleasant. He also is capable of working through pleasurable circumstances such as the enjoyment of interacting with friends or the receipt of an award. Through events such as these, an individual may perhaps gain an increased respect and concern for others or a greater appreciation of life, thus developing toward the Divine nature.

The Divine persuasion operates through several means, including the experience of certain events, as well as the occurrence of various human feelings and thoughts. These different avenues by which the Divine persuasion works, however, do not remain separate from each other. Feelings often overlap with ideas, and ideas are frequently accompanied by feelings. Events may contribute to the development of feelings or thoughts, and the presence of feelings or thoughts may bring about the occurrence of events. What does this mean in regard to the operation of the Divine persuasion? Certainly because of God's interest in us, it must be that God also works through this process. God not only seeks to persuade individuals through particular aspects of human existence such as events, feelings, and thoughts, but he seeks to work through their interaction. In the final analysis, it must be said that God is involved in all of the human situation, seeking to persuade each person toward him.

Numerous illustrations could be given of the presence of the Divine persuasion in the lives of particular individuals, both out of the past and in the present. The lives of many of the characters in the Bible indicate this activity of the Divine, especially major figures such as Moses and Paul. The life of an individual in the history of Christianity that clearly reveals the operation of the Divine persuasion in much of its diversity is that of Saint Augustine.

Augustine was born in Africa in 354 and was raised under the influence of his Christian mother. He spent most of his adult years as a dedicated bishop in Africa, but there was a period in his life between his late teens and early thirties in which he rejected Christianity. During this time he had difficulty controlling his passions, and he accepted a rather hedonistic approach to life. At the same time, he also adopted a materialistic philosophy called Manichaeanism, which to a great extent allowed him to attribute evil to a force outside of himself and to deny responsibility for his weaknesses. Nevertheless, during these years the Divine persuasion was steadily working with his life in several different ways. Through various means such as feelings, thoughts, and events God was encouraging him toward his conversion to Christianity.[8]

In regard to Augustine's feelings during these years of his life, God was particularly able to utilize his guilt, despair, and fear. To some degree Augustine was aware of his sins and was not fully satisfied with the way he was living. He spoke of still having a belief in a Divine judgment and a fear of death. Furthermore, the Divine persuasion operated through Augustine's reflection and his confrontation with new ideas and perspectives. For instance, at one point he came in contact with certain neo-Platonic writings that included certain philosophical similarities with Christianity. These works led to his acceptance of the concept of an immaterial reality and eventually to him reading the New Testament. Additionally, God encouraged Augustine toward himself through numerous events. For example, Augustine interacted with several Christians who were inspirational and at the same time were able to give a reasonable explanation of Christianity. Of course, there was also the dynamic experience in his garden, which served as the final event in his conversion.[9]

The Divine persuasion, therefore, was active in the life of Augustine as he encountered different feelings, thoughts, and events. Again it must be emphasized that God also works through the interaction of these aspects of one's experience, and certainly this was true in Augustine's life. Undoubtedly his feelings made him more susceptible to change and to the adoption of the ideas within Christianity. Moreover, the relationships

---

[8]Aurelius Augustine, *The Confessions of Saint Augustine* (New York: Pocket Books, Inc., 1951) 30-148; Frederick Copleston, *A History of Philosophy* (Garden City: Doubleday and Company, Inc., 1950) 2:55-62.

[9]Augustine, 30-148; Copleston, 55-59.

and discussions that he had with Christians such as Simplicianus obviously stimulated him to think about himself and his life-style. God was
operating through the whole of the circumstances confronting Augustine,
as well as through specific facets of his life. However, this Divine involvement throughout the life of the individual is not confined to the life of
Augustine. This is the way that the Divine seeks to persuade every person
toward a closer relationship with him.

In summary, as human beings we are like all other members of the universe in the sense that we are a part of an interdependent universe and
have a need to share ourselves with others. There is, however, a basic difference between ourselves and other existents. We are a being of freedom
and possibility; therefore, we must decide for ourselves whether we will
affirm or deny the Divine nature as an approach to life. At the same time,
we always exist in a state of conflict since we have a need to be self-giving,
but are inclined to be self-centered and alienated. Consequently, in order
to develop toward the loving attitude that God wants us to have, we must
become involved in the practice of self-denial. This is an exercise encouraged by God in which we reject our narrow personal interests so that
we may be more like the Divine.

With this understanding of the Divine nature and the human situation, it is now appropriate to discuss more specifically our encounter with
the Divine. The question can be raised as to how the human comes into
contact with the Divine. What are the different ways that we have of interacting with God? This question is answered by pointing to the general
categories of the mystical and the ethical, for they are the fundamental
means by which we are able to know the Divine nature. We now turn to
an examination of each of these basic experiences.

Discussion Questions

1. Do we tend to overlook the various ways that we are dependent upon other kinds of beings?

2. What does it mean to grant others intrinsic value? Do you think all beings should be afforded this value?

3. Is it correct to speak of nonhuman beings as having certain rights that we should acknowledge? If so, what do you think is the nature of these rights?

4. Is it possible for us to be personally responsible for our actions if we do not have freedom of choice? Do you think of yourself as being free and responsible for your actions?

5. What exactly does it mean to be alienated from yourself? Does alienation from self necessarily imply alienation from others?

6. What are some examples of possible acts of self-denial toward nonhuman beings besides those that are mentioned in the chapter?

7. How would you describe the operation of the Divine persuasion? What are some instances of the work of the Divine persuasion within your own life?

8. What are the various ways that the Divine persuasion worked in the lives of Moses and Paul? What other Biblical characters especially reveal the presence of the Divine persuasion in their lives?

Suggestions for Further Reading

Augustine, Aurelius. *The Confessions of Saint Augustine*. New York: Pocket Books, Inc., 1951.

Barbour, Ian G. *Technology, Environment, and Human Values*. New York: Praeger Publishers, 1980.

Fromm, Erich. *To Have or To Be*. New York: Harper and Row, 1976.

Hendricks, William L. *The Doctrine of Man*. Nashville: Convention Press, 1977.

Jung, C. G. *Modern Man in Search of a Soul*. New York: Harcourt, Brace, and World, 1933.

Kierkegaard, Søren. *Works of Love*. New York: Harper and Row, 1962.

Marcel, Gabriel. *Man Against Mass Society*. Chicago: Henry Regnery Company, 1952.

May, Rollo. *Man's Search for Himself*. New York: W. W. Norton and Company, 1953.

Niebuhr, Reinhold. *The Nature and Destiny of Man*. New York: Charles Scribner's Sons, 1941.

Rust, Eric C. *Science and Faith: Towards a Theological Understanding of Nature*. New York: Oxford University Press, 1967.

Sartre, Jean-Paul. *Being and Nothingness*. New York: Washington Square Press, 1953.

Schumacher, E. F. *Small is Beautiful*. New York: Harper and Row, 1973.

Tillich, Paul. *The Courage to Be*. New Haven CT: Yale University Press, 1952.

_____. *The Shaking of the Foundations*. New York: Charles Scribner's Sons, 1948.

_____. *Systematic Theology*. Chicago: The University of Chicago Press, 1957.

Tournier, Paul. *The Meaning of Persons*. New York: Harper and Row, 1957.

III

Mystical Experience

This chapter describes a mystical experience as one in which God is experienced in a direct manner so that there is an immediate encounter with the Divine. During this encounter there is a communion between God and man with both the Divine and the human contributing to the experience of Divine love. Even though self-giving love dominates the individual during the mystical relationship, this does not necessarily mean that an attitude of love will be maintained after the experience. In order for this love to continue with the individual, it must be shared with others in some manner.

The Definition of the Experience

There is no single, universally agreed upon definition for "mystical experience," but instead the term is used in a variety of ways. For some it refers to mysterious phenomena associated with such practices as clairvoyance, magic, and the occult, and for others the term denotes hearing voices and seeing visions. There are also those who use it in the broad sense of referring to any type of event that is vague or difficult to explain, while others confine the use of the term to a special state of consciousness that is achieved through particular methods of contemplation.[1]

A basic meaning of the concept is in reference to an immediate awareness of the Divine, which is the way the term will be used in the present discussion. In such an experience the individual may have contact with other material existents, and these existents may provide favorable conditions for the person's encounter with the Divine. In fact, God is actively seeking to encourage those conditions that will provide an opportunity for this encounter, and in this sense God works through other material existents in a mystical experience. In an immediate experience of God, however, this Divine activity through other existents is secondary compared to the central thrust of the encounter. The predominant and essential means by which the Divine is known in this experience is through God's direct communication of himself. In a mystical experience the Divine nature is directly communicated to the individual, and the person has a direct insight into the self-giving love of God.

A large variety of situations exist in which a mystical intuition may take place. Such an experience may occur in association with a prayer or an act of self-reflection. It might also happen as one relates to other people or some other form of life. Still another possible set of circumstances for this experience is one's relationship with physical nature. Interaction with a river, an ocean, or a mountain sometimes provides the context for a mystical encounter with the Divine.

Although a mystical experience may take place in many different situations, there are two principal types that can be distinguished. These two types are referred to by different terms. Walter Stace calls them "the introvertive" and "the extrovertive,"[2] whereas Rudolf Otto labels them the "inward way" and "the way of unity."[3] Still another way of contrasting these two types is by referring to them as "soul-mysticism" and "nature-

---

[1]Walter T. Stace, *The Teachings of the Mystics* (New York: New American Library, 1960) 9-12; Georgia Harkness, *Mysticism, Its Meaning and Message* (Nashville: Abingdon Press, 1973) 18-20.

[2]Stace, 15-23.

[3]Rudolf Otto, *Mysticism, East and West* (New York: Macmillan Publishing Co., 1932) 57-72.

mysticism.)[4] Regardless of the name that might be attached to these forms of mysticism, the distinction is between a concentration upon the Divine that is directed toward the inward self and one that is directed toward the external world.

The inward or introvertive type of mysticism is grounded in introspection. The person looks into the self, and this provides a basis for the mystical intuition. At the same time, outward things are for the most part excluded from consciousness. Perceptions of material objects are either not involved at all, or they are involved only in a highly secondary manner. The individual turns to the inner self for communication with the Divine and does not give attention to the external world.[5]

Various expressions of introvertive mysticism were set forth by John Ruysbroeck, who lived in Flanders in Western Europe during the thirteenth and fourteenth centuries. The following statement from his writings serves as an example of this inward type of mysticism:

> At times, the inward man performs his introspection simply, according to the fruitive tendency, above all activity and above all virtues, through a simple inward gazing in the fruition of love. And here he meets God without intermediary.[6]

The other principal kind of mystical experience is extrovertive in nature in that it is focused outward into the external world. In this case sense perception is utilized as a means toward having a mystical intuition. The person looks outward and recognizes the presence of the Divine throughout nature. This experience is, therefore, a vision of the unity of all things in the world. That is, because of the affirmation of God's existence through or with each object and event, nature is viewed as a whole. All things are seen as being in unity with each other because everything is said to include the presence of the Divine. As a result of this perspective, those who have this type of encounter may at times refer to the world as the "Whole," "All," or "One."[7]

---

[4]F. C. Happold, *Mysticism: A Study and an Anthology* (Baltimore: Penguin Books, 1963) 43-45.

[5]Stace, 15, 17-23; Otto, 59-60.

[6]Happold, 287.

[7]Stace, 15-17; Otto, 60-72.

Friedrich Schleiermacher was a German philosopher who lived in the eighteenth and nineteenth centuries. Although he is not usually labeled a mystic, his writings do contain numerous expressions of extrovertive mysticism. The following is an example from one of his works of this type of mysticism:

> The contemplation of the pious is the immediate consciousness of the universal existence of all finite things, in and through the infinite and of all temporal things in and through the Eternal. . . . Wherefore it is a life in the infinite nature of the Whole, in the One and in the All, in God, having and possessing all things in God, and God in all.[8]

In introvertive mysticism the individual focuses upon the inward self, and in extrovertive mysticism the individual looks out into the world. Even though there are many mystical experiences that are clearly either introvertive or extrovertive in nature, it should not be assumed that these types are always completely separate from each other. A person, for instance, may be in contact with the outside world in some manner and at the same time be involved in introspection. This may lead to a mystical experience that participates in both the introvertive and extrovertive forms, or it may result in introvertive and extrovertive intuitions that adjoin or overlap. In addition, it is possible for the presence of one of these types of mysticism to lead into the occurrence of the other. For example, an extrovertive experience may stimulate an individual toward introspection and an introvertive encounter. Therefore, the introvertive and extrovertive forms of mysticism are not necessarily sharply divided from each other, but may be joined together in some fashion.

The Contribution of the Divine and the Human

These mystical experiences are possible because God is constantly reaching out to man and seeking to transform him into Divine love. Without God's willingness to extend himself to man, there would not be any mystical encounters, regardless of what man tried to do to foster this occurrence. The necessity of the Divine in a mystical experience is emphasized in the following statement by John Ruysbroeck:

---

[8]Friedrich Schleiermacher, *On Religion: Speeches to Its Cultured Despisers* (New York: Harper and Row, 1958) 36.

This essential union of our spirit with God does not exist in itself, but it dwells in God and it flows forth from God, and it depends upon God, and it returns to God as to its Eternal Origin. And in this wise it has never been, nor shall be, separated from God; for this union is within us by our naked nature, and, were this nature to be separated from God, it would fall into pure nothingness.[9]

In order for a mystical experience to take place, God must in some way present himself to the individual. It is the case, however, that God is willing to do this, for as already indicated, God has a caring nature and is willing to share himself with man. He directs his empathy toward each person as well as toward the other beings in the universe. God is always involved in empathizing with each person so that he will know every life situation, and with this knowledge he is able to provide assistance for human needs. This identification with an individual also allows for the possibility of a mystical experience. That is, it is empathy that serves as the Divine presence in this encounter. Through empathy God projects himself into the person's life and makes himself available for a direct relationship.

In addition to this Divine contribution, there is also a human element involved in a mystical experience. This human element is the appropriation of the Divine presence by the individual. Before a mystical experience can take place, the individual must receive the Divine love in a manner that allows God to have an effect upon his being. This demands that the individual have a degree of tolerance toward the Divine. In other words, the person must to some extent be receptive toward the Divine attitude of love. There must be a tendency toward this attitude or at least an openness toward the possibility of its truth. This tolerance, however, must be present just prior to the mystical experience. An individual could have this perspective at one point in time and not have it at some other point. Even the individual who has made self-giving love the predominant approach of his existence is still to some degree intermittent in his outlook. There are occasions in which he is closed to new experiences with the Divine.

Although this tolerance is necessary before an individual is able to appropriate Divine love, this alone is not sufficient. There must be circum-

---

[9]Happold, 286.

stances surrounding the person's existence that afford him the opportunity
to give attention to the Divine. There must be a chance for the individual's being to be directed toward that which he does not usually experience. The presence of other people, for example, may serve to prevent an
individual from having a mystical experience. A person is not able to be
alert to this type of Divine participation when he is preoccupied with
communicating with others. For a mystical experience to take place, it is
often beneficial for an individual to be alone, but if he is accompanied by
others, he must be able to concentrate upon his own situation and relationship to God. In addition, a person needs to have sufficient time to appropriate Divine love. This time is not present, for instance, when an
individual is heavily involved in performing mundane tasks.

This human element in a mystical experience demands a proper outlook on the part of the individual as well as favorable circumstances for
the reception of the Divine. It should be noted, however, that this so-
called human element is not purely man's endeavor, for even at this point
God has a contribution to make to the experience. God is also working in
the process by which human perspectives are developed and human situations arise. He seeks to encourage an individual to adopt a tolerant attitude and at the same time attempts to lead him toward favorable
circumstances for concentration.

This additional Divine contribution to the occurrence of mystical experiences is yet another aspect of the operation of the Divine persuasion.
It was previously pointed out that God uses various means in an attempt
to persuade individuals toward the Divine attitude. An example of how
this Divine persuasion works in regard to a mystical experience is the person's need from time to time to reflect upon himself and the meaning of
his relationships in the world. Such acts are often helpful for coping with
life and are frequently refreshing by offering a respite from one's usual activities. Furthermore, through the positive outcome of these acts, the individual is motivated toward similar acts in the future. At the same time,
these acts may contribute to a mystical encounter with the Divine. The
acts themselves set up advantageous conditions for this kind of experience.

The Nature of the Experience

A mystical experience consists of the presence of Divine empathy and
a human response that is assisted by the Divine. Moreover, the nature of

this experience is one in which the individual has an intimate encounter with the Divine. This encounter is often spoken of as a union of the Divine and the human, and certainly there is a sense in which the individual is joined with God. During the experience the person interacts with the Divine and feels the presence of God. This encounter, however, can never be one of complete unity with the Divine because of the element of human alienation. Estrangement from God is a state of human existence and can never be entirely removed. Even in a mystical experience, man's being is not one of Divine love in the complete sense. It is true that during this experience love becomes dominant within the individual, but it is never able to attain an absolute status as is the case with the Divine. Only the love of God's own being is ever pure and without limitation.

The part that the past plays in an individual's life indicates that a mystical experience can never be one of complete unity with God. John Cobb points this out in the following statement about this type of experience:

> Experientially speaking, it may well be understood as an experience of union with God, even though, philosophically speaking, actual identity must be denied.
> An experience of communion is differentiated from that of union by the continuing self-identity of the human person. The human occasion continues to inherit from its personal past to an important degree.[10]

That is, an individual's past serves as a clue to his personal identity. As a person has experiences, he seeks to relate them to himself and give them a meaningful interpretation. These experiences and their accompanying interpretations provide the individual with his self-identity. They form the content for the individual's understanding of himself and his world. At the same time, they are the means by which the person is able to cope with his present. Each person is constantly drawing upon these past experiences and interpretations to understand the new events in his life. Therefore, any new experience must have reference to the individual's personal past. This means that the person's response to the Divine during a mystical experience must be a response that utilizes past experiences. Because of the necessary connection between past experiences and per-

---

[10]John B. Cobb, Jr., *A Christian Natural Theology* (Philadelphia: The Westminster Press, 1965) 234-35.

sonal identity, the individual's self-identity must be present throughout a mystical experience. Even though during this experience an individual may feel as though his being is completely absorbed into the Divine, this loss of self, nevertheless, does not occur. As Cobb indicates, the relationship in such an experience is not one in which the individual becomes fully identical with the Divine, but one in which God shares himself with the individual. Instead of being a union between God and man, it is a relationship of communion between the Divine and human.[11]

Since a mystical experience is one in which God shares himself with man, this means that it must be an experience of Divine love. In a mystical experience, that which the individual is joined with is self-giving love. The individual responds to Divine empathy and allows it to become a part of himself. As a result, there is a transformation of the individual's being into a Divine outlook. This alteration in man during a mystical experience is pointed out by St. John of the Cross, a sixteenth-century mystic. Although he recognized that the human does not become identical to the Divine, he emphasized that the various functions of the self take on a Divine approach during the experience. For example, he says that

> . . . the understanding, which before this union understood in a natural way with the strength and vigor of its natural light, is now moved and informed by another principle, that of the supernatural light of God, and has been changed into the Divine, for its understanding and that of God are now both one. And the will, which aforetime loved after the manner of death, that is to say, meanly and with its natural affection, has now been changed into the life of Divine love; . . .[12]

Accompanying this transformation during a mystical experience is a weakening of the self-centeredness within the individual. The narrow selfish outlook becomes ineffectual, and the Divine gains the major influence. This aspect of a mystical experience was given attention by a mystical movement in Islam called Sufism, which acquired importance in the ninth century A.D. and continued for several centuries thereafter. One of the emphases of the Sufis was the possibility for one to have an ecstatic experience of the Divine without the interference of the self-centered

[11]Ibid., 233-35.

[12]Happold, 365.

ego.[13] The following statement by a Persian Sufi named Jami is an example of this emphasis:

> And in this course thou must persevere until He mingles Himself with thy soul, and thine own individual existence passes out of thy sight. Then, if thou regardest thyself, it is He whom thou art regarding: if thou speakest of thyself, it is He of whom thou art speaking. The relative has become the Absolute, and "I am the Truth" is equivalent to "He is the Truth."[14]

The Sufis tended to exaggerate the extent to which one's egocentric character is able to be overcome during this kind of experience. It is apparent from reading this passage and other statements by the Sufis that they thought of this relationship as involving a complete loss of self as well as an unqualified union with the Divine. Of course, this aspect of their view must be rejected because, as already indicated, personal estrangement, along with one's self-identity, does continue throughout the encounter. It is correct to say, however, that this experience has a diminishing effect upon the narrow side of the self. That is, during the experience, the Divine nature gains a primary influence upon the self, and there is a significant decline in the influence of the alienated and self-centered dimension of the individual.

During a mystical experience the Divine transforms the individual so that love exercises control and the self-centered nature is weakened. In addition, the individual experiences the feeling of being more than he has been before. He has a sense of being filled with something superior to himself, something that is to some degree uplifting. There is an inner joy that is present, which is enlivening and refreshing, and along with this joy there is a general sense of gratitude and tranquility. During a mystical experience the individual gains a large degree of appreciation and contentment toward the nature of existence and toward himself. St. John of the Cross compares this experience of God by the mystic with the experience of a woman on the day of her betrothal. In each case a kind of love that is primarily unselfish in character is central to the experience, and this love gives rise to the sentiments of joy, peace, and appreciation. At one

---

[13]Ibid., 249-51; Stace, 201-203.

[14]Happold, 259.

point he describes both the engaged woman and the mystical soul in the following manner:

> And upon this happy day, not only is there an end of the soul's former vehement yearnings and plaints of love, but, being adorned with the good things which I am describing, she enters into an estate of peace and delight and sweetness of love wherein she does naught else but relate and sing the wonders of her Beloved, which she knows and enjoys in Him, by means of the aforementioned union of her betrothal. . . .[15]

The Results of the Experience

A mystical experience, therefore, is one in which Divine love is permitted to become a part of the individual. This love dominates the person's being, and this produces feelings of joy, peace, and gratitude. An experience of this kind can serve to encourage the individual in the direction of a more permanent self-giving approach to life. It may give the individual a beginning appreciation of Divine love, or if this is already present, the individual may be stimulated toward accepting this love more tenaciously and practicing it more extensively. The experience itself, however, does not necessarily imply this sort of result, for it is possible for the individual to reject this love soon after the experience. Even though during the experience this attitude does take control, it may not continue for any considerable length of time afterwards. The individual may revert to a former attitude or soon have new experiences that influence him toward some other outlook.

An example of a conflicting attitude with the Divine nature that may develop after a mystical experience is one that has an aversion toward this present existence. Søren Kierkegaard claims that this kind of attitude is characteristic of persons who have had mystical experiences. He says that the mystic does not understand that history exists as a gift of God and that each person has a responsibility to become involved in it and seek to contribute to its development. Instead, the temporal is viewed as being merely a probation period in which, for the most part, the infinite and finite spirits are separated and in which the individual is being tested and

---

[15]Ibid., 363.

tried by the Divine. The only significance that the temporal has for the mystic is that it is a time of trial and that it makes possible momentary encounters with the Divine.[16]

According to Kierkegaard, this attitude by the mystic indicates a disdain for God's love, since it is God's love that has provided this existence. He goes on to say:

> Who will deny that a man shall love God with all his heart and with all his mind, yea, that he is not only to do this but that to do it is blessedness itself? From this, however, it by no means follows that the mystic is to disdain the reality of existence to which God has assigned him, for thereby he really disdains God's love or requires a different expression of it from that which God is willing to give.[17]

Furthermore, claims Kierkegaard, this attitude leads the mystic to isolate himself from others. He chooses the solitary life and the life of religious contemplation, and as a result he ignores his responsibilities toward others. Brief moments of isolation may be beneficial to the inwardness of an individual and, therefore, contribute to his earthly relationships. In the case of the mystic, however, isolation becomes a sickness because it is made to be a way of life.[18] Kierkegaard insists that

> He who devotes himself one-sidedly to the mystical life becomes at last so alien to all men that every relationship, even the tenderest, the most heartfelt, becomes indifferent to him. It is not in this sense one is to love God more dearly than father and mother; God is not so self-loving as that, neither is He a poet who wishes to torment men with the most frightful collisions—and hardly could a more frightful thing be conceived than that there might be a collision between love for God and love for the persons for whom love has been planted by Him in our hearts.[19]

Thus, Kierkegaard argues that the mystic dislikes this existence and also neglects his responsibilities toward others. Moreover, this attitude is in-

---

[16]Søren Kierkegaard, *Either/Or* (Garden City: Doubleday and Company, 1959) 2:249, 254-55.

[17]Ibid., 248.

[18]Ibid., 247, 249, 251.

[19]Ibid., 249.

cluded within Kierkegaard's concept of mysticism. That is, he thinks of a mystic as one who has this perspective, and without it the person would not really be a mystic.

Nevertheless, this attitude does not necessarily accompany mystical experience as it has been defined in this chapter. Certainly there are those who have a direct experience with the Divine that at the same time are able to avoid this kind of outlook. Walter Stace agrees that this attitude does not always result from this kind of experience, and he indicates that some mystics have even stressed the need for mystical experiences to be followed by a high moral life. He says:

> It is sometimes asserted that mysticism is merely an escape from life and from its duties and responsibilities. . . . It is possible that there have been mystics who deserved this kind of condemnation. To treat the bliss of the mystical consciousness as an end in itself is certainly a psychological possibility. And no doubt there have been men who have succumbed to this temptation. But this attitude is not the mystic ideal, and it is severely condemned by those who are most representative of the mystics themselves. . . .[20]

Although the mystical experience does not always give rise to this attitude, it no doubt does in some cases. This points to the fact that the love that comes to an individual through a mystical experience may not be lasting. It may soon be replaced by some other approach to life. Of course, even if the individual continues in the affirmation of self-giving after the experience, it may not be something that he is able to practice. He may sincerely want to extend love to others in his relationships, but he may not be able to do so because of a weak character. He may be unable to control his physical desires and emotions, or he may not have the courage to act on the basis of his own will.

There is a need for the love of God to be maintained within the individual after a mystical experience, since it is this love that enables the individual to achieve a fulfilling existence. In order for this love to continue, the individual must be willing to outwardly express this love. He must be willing to share this love with others. One means available to the individual for expressing his love is his direct relationship with God. In

---

[20]Stace, 26.

this expression the individual utilizes the love that the Divine has given him and extends it back toward God. He gives himself to God through his appreciation and trust toward what the Divine has done for him and continues to do. He devotes himself to God.

There are several ways that this devotion can take place. One of these is the practice of praise and thanksgiving. In these acts the individual gives affirmation to the nature and activity of the Divine. He demonstrates that he agrees with the principles that God upholds and the purposes that he is seeking to carry out. He also expresses gratitude for what God is and what he is doing in his own life and the rest of the universe. Another practice of devotion to God is that of seeking forgiveness. In this act the individual indicates that his desire is to be more like the Divine and that he has confidence in God's ability to help him attain this. He asks God to accept him even though he thinks of himself as having been involved in wrongdoing. He communicates to God his belief that he has violated God's intention for him, and he apologizes for what he has done and tells God he would like to begin or reconstitute a close relationship with him. There is another type of devotion that reveals both a will on the part of the individual to be like God and a sense of trust in God's capacity to help. In this case the individual seeks to acquire strength and guidance for his life. He sets forth the desire that his thoughts, words, and deeds be those that are sanctioned by the Divine, and he asks God to aid him in understanding and implementing the Divine will for his life.

One way, therefore, by which an individual is able to share the love coming from a mystical experience is by extending it directly back to the Divine. This expression of love, however, is not sufficient by itself to enable an individual to continue in the Divine love of a mystical experience. A person must be willing to share this love through his relationships in the universe. This expression of love is part of the ethical realm of existence. Before giving attention in the next chapter to an investigation of this ethical dimension of life, it is first necessary to summarize what has been said about the mystical experience of the Divine.

In a mystical experience God is known through a direct communication with him in which there is an immediate awareness of self-giving love by the individual. This experience consists of both the presence of the Divine and the appropriate human response, but God is involved even in the human aspect of the encounter in that he encourages man toward the attitude and circumstances that are conducive for the experience. In addition, instead of being an experience of complete union with the Divine, it is one of communion between God and man in which self-giving love dominates the individual. This love may not continue after the encounter, for it is possible that the individual may develop some other outlook. In order for this loving attitude to be maintained after the experience, the person must be willing to share this love with others.

Discussion Questions

1. What part does human initiative and effort play in the occurrence of a mystical experience? Should a person seek to do certain things in order to help bring about this kind of experience?

2. In our relationship with God, is it ever possible for the human element to distort the Divine involvement so that the spirit of the Divine is not genuinely experienced?

3. Are there any experiences that may be similar to mystical experiences in certain ways, but which may not actually be mystical experiences in the true sense?

4. Are there any reasons why it might be difficult for Americans to have a mystical experience? If so, what reasons would you mention?

5. Do you agree that a mystical experience is more a matter of communion with God than union with him?

6. If you have ever had a mystical experience, how would you describe what you felt and thought when it occurred? Would you use such concepts as joy, peace, and gratitude in your description?

7. Do you agree that it is possible to have a mystical experience and then soon develop an attitude that is largely opposed to the Divine nature?

Suggestions for Further Reading

Buber, Martin. *I and Thou*. New York: Charles Scribner's Sons, 1958.

Cobb, John B. *A Christian Natural Theology*. Philadelphia: The Westminster Press, 1965.

Deissmann, Adolf. *Paul, A Study in Social and Religious History*. New York: Harper and Row, 1912.

Happold, F. C. *Mysticism: A Study and an Anthology*. Baltimore: Penguin Books, 1963.

Harkness, Georgia. *Mysticism, Its Meaning and Message*. Nashville: Abingdon Press, 1973.

James, William. *The Varieties of Religious Experience*. New York: Longmans, Green and Co., 1928.

Katz, Steven T., ed. *Mysticism and Philosophical Analysis*. New York: Oxford University Press, 1978.

Kierkegaard, Søren. *Either/Or*. Garden City NY: Doubleday and Company, 1959.

Otto, Rudolf. *The Idea of the Holy*. London: Oxford University Press, 1923.

——————————. *Mysticism, East and West*. New York: Macmillan Publishing Co., 1932.

Schleiermacher, Friedrich. *The Christian Faith*. Edinburgh: T. and T. Clark, 1928.

——————————. *On Religion: Speeches to Its Cultured Despisers*. New York: Harper and Row, 1958.

Stace, Walter T. *The Teachings of the Mystics*. New York: New American Library, 1960.

Underhill, Evelyn. *The Essentials of Mysticism and Other Essays*. New York: E. P. Dutton and Co., 1920.

——————————. *Practical Mysticism*. New York: E. P. Dutton and Co., 1915.

IV

Ethical Experience

In this chapter the meaning of the ethical experience of the Divine is examined. This kind of experience is defined as an encounter with God through our relationships in the universe. Within these relationships there are certain ethical responsibilities that we have toward others and toward ourselves. Our responsibilities toward others include duties toward other human beings, nonhuman life, and inanimate objects, with human life being given priority over the other types of beings. Our responsibilities toward ourselves consist of the obligations that we have toward others along with some immediate duties that we have toward ourselves.

Our Responsibilities Toward Others

Mystical experience is one way that we have of knowing the Divine, but this direct encounter is not our only means of access to God. We can have what can be called ethical experiences of God in which the Divine is encountered through the finite. That is, another means by which we are able to receive God's love is through our interaction with the material beings in the universe. This includes relationships with not only other beings but also with ourselves.

In our relationships with others, God shares himself and provides for our needs. The extension of this Divine love comes through our contact with several different kinds of beings including plants, animals, and inanimate objects. It was pointed out in chapter two that there are many ways that these nonhuman beings give assistance to our existence. They not only provide us with certain fundamental ingredients for life such as food, water, and oxygen, but they make other contributions such as clothing, shelter, companionship, and pleasurable experiences of beauty. Of course, we must not overlook the love that comes to us through our experiences with other human beings. There are numerous examples of how other people contribute to our existence. Parents share themselves by giving birth, nourishment, and guidance to their children. Certain people provide an individual with friendship and companionship, and others give instructions that are necessary for understanding and coping with life. Still others provide an individual with goods and services that are helpful in meeting everyday needs. In these ways and others a person confronts Divine love through human relationships.

We are able to encounter the Divine through our relationships with these various types of beings. Every person has experienced God's love through relationships in each of these areas. All have benefited from the gifts and sacrifices of other persons, nonhuman life, and the inanimate realm. At the same time, these contributions from others point to man's moral responsibilities to the rest of existence. Since an individual's life depends upon the activities of others, he ought to value and assist their existence. A person should to some extent be considerate and sacrificing toward others in order to preserve his own physical well-being.

The protection of our own life is not the only reason to be self-giving toward the various spheres of existence. As previously stated, each of us is a part of the interrelated system of the universe, which demands self-giving from its constituents. The welfare of the whole is maintained by the sacrifices of each area of existence, and as a member of nature, man must be willing to share himself for the betterment of the universe. In addition, we should carry out this attitude because it allows us to gain a form of unity with others, God, and our own selves. It enables us to be joined with others in healthy relationships and to follow what God wills in these relationships. At the same time, we are able to achieve a sense of fulfillment within ourselves. There is an inner feeling of satisfaction that comes to one who shares himself with others. It is the satisfaction of being responsible toward others and properly joined with others.

This personal reward of unity and fulfillment indicates another aspect of one's ethical experience of the Divine. This aspect is the acquisition of Divine love that results from performing one's duties toward others. God's love is encountered as one receives from others in the universe, but it is also experienced as one gives in return. Furthermore, because ethical experience contains both of these elements, this means that the possible motives and consequences surrounding our moral responsibilities toward others must be understood in two ways. On the one hand, there is the more obvious sense in which our deeds can assist others and their deeds can assist us. On the other hand, there is the sense in which we can benefit from carrying out our obligations. After all, through self-giving we not only gain unity with others and inward satisfaction, but we provide support to the whole of which we are a part. Therefore, as Friedrich Nietzsche has pointed out, loving actions on behalf of others carry with them an egoistic quality. The person is meeting his own needs at the same time that he is giving aid to another.[1]

Thus, when ethical obligations toward others are performed by the individual, God's love is experienced through certain personal rewards as well as through the benefits that come from other beings. What can be said about those who do not carry out their moral responsibilities toward others? To answer this question it is necessary to return to the notion of alienation. Failure in one's responsibilities toward other beings brings about some degree of estrangement in one's relationships with others and with God along with some sense of separation from what one ought to be.

A question that arises regarding the nature of alienation in one's relationships with others is whether it is possible to be alienated from one type of being without being alienated from all of them. For example, does being alienated from nonhuman life imply that one is also alienated from other human beings? Immanuel Kant deals with this issue when he discusses the relation between a person's treatment of animals and his treatment of other human beings. He says that "he who is cruel to animals becomes hard also in his dealings with man. We can judge the heart of a

---

[1]Friedrich Nietzsche, *Human, All-Too-Human* (New York: Russell and Russell, Inc., 1964) 1:134-36.

man by his treatment of animals."² It is no doubt true that what Kant says at this point is often the case, but it does not seem to always hold. One may think that he has very few if any responsibilities to nonhuman realms of existence. He may not recognize the contributions of these other beings, or because of his ability to overpower and dominate them, he may exploit them for his own self-interest. This individual, however, may at the same time be highly considerate and sacrificing in his relationships with other people. He may have a high standard of responsibility toward humanity and be faithful in adhering to that standard. It is also possible for an individual to be alienated from other people but not from nonhuman beings. An individual might have a special interest in nonhuman spheres or have suffered undue disappointment and hardship from other persons. Consequently, he might be understanding and giving in his relationships with nonhuman life and inanimate objects, but apprehensive and even hostile toward other human beings. Therefore, it does appear that it is possible for one to be estranged from some but not all kinds of beings. The way one treats one type of being is not always an indication of how he treats all beings.

The Priority of Human Beings

We have moral responsibilities toward other human beings, nonhuman life, and inanimate existence, and alienation occurs when there is a failure in these responsibilities. At this point it is necessary to consider the nature of our moral responsibilities toward others. What can be said about the way we should treat others? Fundamental in this regard is the perspective that was emphasized in chapter two in which all beings are treated as having value in themselves. This means that other people are to be thought of as having worth regardless of their material wealth, social position, or educational level. They must be respected simply because they are people even though they may not be able to make any significant contribution to society or to our own lives. Furthermore, this implies that all nonhuman life and inanimate objects should be approached with consideration and respect. They must be appreciated as existing beings in the universe even if they do not assist one's own life in a direct or obvious manner.

---

²Immanuel Kant, *Lectures on Ethics* (New York: Harper and Row, 1963) 240.

Even if all types of beings are afforded intrinsic value, an issue that still has to be explored is the question of priority. Should man give priority in his decisions to human beings over other kinds of beings, or should he give equal consideration to each realm of existence? James Gustafson emphasizes that the typical approach to this issue in the history of Christianity has been an anthropocentric stance. That is, there has been a strong tradition within Christianity that has assumed that God's will for the universe is centered in the fulfillment of man. Man's welfare is looked upon as being the supreme concern of the Divine, and this viewpoint has served as a justification for the way that man relates to the other beings in the universe. Other existing things are basically understood as being in the service of humanity.[3] Gustafson describes this tradition in the following way:

> Rather than the "cosmos" being the object of divine governance, with human beings as a part of that, the well-being of man is understood to be the supreme object of divine governance, and the order of nature is understood to exist for the sake of man. . . . Happily, for this tradition, as for almost all Christian thought, the rest of the creation was understood to be in the service of our species. With our natural orientation toward our fulfillment, and with the coincidence of the "hierarchy of being" with a hierarchy of value, human beings are supreme in both. The rest of the natural order is purposively directed toward the fulfillment of human life.[4]

Peter Singer also discusses the question of how human beings have understood their relationship to nonhuman existents. He argues that the term "speciesist" is applicable to most people in their outlook toward the various beings in the universe. He says that the use of animals in experimentation and for food indicates that most persons are biased in favor of their own species. The majority of human beings are speciesists in that they treat other beings as merely a means to satisfy personal pleasures and to assist the human species.[5] Singer states that

---

[3]James Gustafson, *Ethics From a Theocentric Perspective* (Chicago: The University of Chicago Press, 1981) 1:88-99.

[4]Ibid., 91-92.

[5]Peter Singer, "All Animals Are Equal," *Animal Rights and Human Obligations*, ed. Tom Regan and Peter Singer (Englewood Cliffs: Prentice-Hall, 1976) 153-62.

The racist violates the principle of equality by giving greater weight to the interests of members of his own race, when there is a clash between their interests and the interests of those of another race. Similarly the speciesist allows the interests of his own species to override the greater interests of other species. The pattern is the same in each case. Most human beings are speciesists.[6]

Therefore, both Gustafson and Singer contend that a widely accepted position on this issue of man's relationship to other beings is one that gives priority to humans. Moreover, there is no doubt that both of them are correct in what they claim at this point. It has usually been thought within Christianity, as Gustafson indicates, that God's will for the universe is man-centered, and also, as Singer says, most people are speciesist in that greater attention is given to the interests of the human species. It still has to be determined, however, whether this should be the case. Should we think of God's concern for the universe as being centered in man? Should we give priority to human beings over other types of beings?

In this regard, it must be acknowledged that Gustafson is right when he says that God's supreme concern is directed toward all creation and not simply toward man.[7] As he says,

> If one's basic theological perception is of a Deity who rules all of creation, and one's basic perception of life in history and nature is one of patterns of interdependence, then the good that God values must be more inclusive than one's normal perceptions of what is good for me, what is good for my community, and even what is good for the human species.[8]

The Divine purpose extends to the whole of the universe, and God is concerned with maintaining what is good for that whole. Man is a part of God's universe, and as such is a part of God's purpose and a recipient of God's love, but God's will for man and the love that man receives must not be thought of as being isolated from the rest of existence. God's involvement with man must be understood in terms of the full context of

---

[6]Ibid., 154.

[7]Gustafson, 96-113.

[8]Ibid., 96.

the Divine relationship to our interdependent universe and all of the beings within it.

Since God's supreme interest is in the welfare of the entire universe, human beings should also have this as their major concern. Each person should be dedicated to promoting the well-being of all existence. Certainly this means that we must recognize the interdependence of all beings in the universe, but it also means that we must grant other beings greater consideration than we have often given them in the past. We must strive to avoid polluting the environment and exploiting other forms of life. For instance, we must refrain from performing cruel or uncalled-for experiments on animals, killing animals for our own amusement, or confining them to highly restrictive cages for long periods of time. But does this mean that other beings should be treated in an equal way with humans? It is true that other kinds of beings deserve greater consideration than they have usually been given, but should they receive equal consideration with man? There are those who argue that there are at least some types of beings that should be extended equal treatment with man. For example, Singer claims that a person should give animals equal consideration with that of human beings. Since animals are beings that are capable of suffering and happiness, he says their interests should be given equal regard.[9] He claims that

> If a being suffers, there can be no moral justification for refusing to take that suffering into consideration. No matter what the nature of the being, the principle of equality requires that its suffering be counted equally with the like suffering—in so far as rough comparison can be made—of any other being. If a being is not capable of suffering, or of experiencing enjoyment or happiness, there is nothing to be taken into account.[10]

In contrast to Singer's position, it must be insisted that even animals should not be given equal consideration with man. Although the supreme concern of the Divine is the good of all of his creation and not merely the well-being of man, this does not mean that he considers all types of beings, or even some, to have equal significance with man. There is still

---

[9]Singer, 148-62.

[10]Ibid., 154.

a certain sense of priority that man has over other beings, and this priority is indicated by the dominion over nature that the Divine has bestowed upon man. As already pointed out, God has chosen us to have a special position in the universe. He has made us the manager over his creation, and it is this major responsibility that justifies our priority. That is, this priority is justified by the large potential that we have for contributing to the whole of existence. We have the ability to furnish God with a high level of assistance as he provides for the welfare of the universe.

Because of this special role in the universe, human beings should be viewed as taking priority over the particular beings of the other areas of existence. Even when this priority is acknowledged, it still has to be interpreted. What is the meaning of this priority in terms of our life-style and relationships to others? One facet of this meaning is the preference that should usually be granted human beings in the various choices that are made between different types of beings. Greater attention should be given to the needs of human beings over those of other beings in the distribution of such things as protection, medical care, food, and water. Of course, this aspect of human priority should not be used as a rationale for the unnecessary mistreatment of other beings; nevertheless, there is a degree of human priority that should be followed at this point.

This priority for human beings also means that we have the right to utilize the various resources of the universe in order to sustain our lives and provide ourselves with security and comfort. We are justified when we use such items as air, water, food from plants and animals, wood, and metals in a manner that will contribute to our welfare. At the same time, however, there is no justification for the waste of these resources. In fact, societies as a whole as well as particular individuals have a responsibility to assist in the wise and constructive use of their resources. Societies should encourage the recycling of resources and set guidelines to guard against wasteful practices. Moreover, individuals must be aware of the significance of their relationship to resources and be willing to maintain prudence and self-control in their use of them.

Another implication of this priority is our right to protect ourselves from injury or death. We are justified in altering nature in some fashion or in hurting some form of life if these actions are necessary in order to maintain our health. For example, we have the right to change the flow of a river to keep it from flooding a community or to kick a dog when it threatens to bite us. This priority, however, does not allow us to have a casual approach to nature or to cause needless harm to other forms of life. We do not have the right, for instance, to cut down trees just to see them fall or to shoot animals just to see them writhe in pain and die.

Our Responsibilities Toward Ourselves

Acknowledgment of our responsibilities toward other people, non-human life, and inanimate existence must be modified with the understanding that human beings should receive priority over other types of beings. Furthermore, it should be pointed out that these obligations toward others can also be viewed as part of an individual's obligations toward himself. At the same time that an individual is being self-giving toward others, he is also being self-giving toward himself in providing what he needs in these relationships. This is not the only way that an individual must carry out self-giving toward himself. Each person is also responsible for his immediate relationships with himself. As an individual selects his actions, he has the responsibility of taking his own self into consideration. He must seek to treat himself in a manner that will promote his health and well-being.

This immediate relationship with oneself includes several responsibilities. One of these is what can be referred to as individuation. This is our responsibility to become a separate and distinct person who is capable of having feelings, ideas, and goals that are one's own. Through individuation the person acquires the ability to think and act autonomously. This is not to say that the person no longer associates with others or listens to them. It is to say that the person is willing to have his own thoughts and to disagree with others when it becomes necessary. Herbert Anderson indicates that individuation is important for each person, and in order for it to develop, the person must break away from parental dependency.[11] He says:

> As we grow up our physical survival depends less and less on our parents. We learn to walk, cross the street, talk, go to school, take care of ourselves more and more. If, however, we continue to depend on our parents for self-definition and self-esteem, the process of individuation is tar-

---

[11]Herbert Anderson, "The Family Under Stress: A Crisis of Purpose," *Moral Issues and Christian Response*, ed. Paul Jersild and Dale Johnson (New York: Holt, Rinehart and Winston, 1971) 120-22.

nished. We spend time and energy seeking their approval, living up to their expectations, worrying whether our feelings are acceptable or the decision we made was right, and failing through it all to gain a sense of our autonomy. We may reach physical maturity well socialized and eager to accommodate others and still not be individuated. Cutting loose from the emotional mooring of our infancy is a life-long process that is in the interest of self-definition. That process of separation is inescapable to the beginning of life.[12]

Another responsibility in our direct relationship with ourselves is that of socialization. We must be willing to interact with others and share ourselves with them. Although this quality is often presented as a responsibility that we have to others and the community, it also must be understood as an obligation that we have to ourselves. Social interaction is of benefit to our lives as well as to others.

Herbert Anderson emphasizes that a person should adhere to both individuation and socialization. Certainly this is not an easy accomplishment, for there is often tension between the two and a tendency for one to be maintained without the other. Nevertheless, personal uniqueness and community must function together in the life of the individual. When these elements are both present, it not only aids the particular person, but it contributes to the vitality and welfare of society as a whole.[13]

A further responsibility in one's immediate relationship with oneself is the duty to protect and care for the body. This would obligate one to meet the health needs of the body, such as adequate sleep, exercise, and nourishment, and to avoid abusing the body, for example, through the misuse of drugs. Of course, these responsibilities to the body would at times be overridden by other responsibilities that one has to oneself and others. Nonetheless, it should be recognized that these bodily duties are ethical responsibilities, which should be obeyed under most circumstances.

We have a personal responsibility to develop our mental capacity. This would include abilities such as reading, writing, analysis, relational thinking, critical thinking, creativity, and the use of our memory. This is not to say that each person must acquire the same degree of efficiency in

---

[12]Ibid., 121.

[13]Ibid., 119-22.

each of these abilities or that each person must develop his or her mental capacity through the same means such as formal education. It is to say that these are mental skills that can be learned and improved through experience and training and that each person has an obligation to himself to work on developing at least some of these. The improvement of these abilities not only opens up broader opportunities of service to others and to society, but it enhances the person's individual existence by encouraging such attributes as self-awareness, self-respect, self-confidence and personal courage.

There are, therefore, some particular responsibilities that accompany one's immediate relationship with oneself. It is interesting to note that there are consequences associated with these immediate responsibilities to oneself that are similar in nature to those that are related to one's responsibilities to others. Like one's relationships to others, there is a sense of inner fulfillment that is derived from carrying out these direct obligations to oneself. There is also an experience of unity that can result from following these responsibilities, but in this case, it is predominantly a feeling of unity with oneself. In addition, failure in these responsibilities causes a form of alienation within the individual. Even though this alienation may result in an estrangement from others and from God, it is primarily an estrangement from oneself. It is centered in one's relationship to oneself with a separation from one's true self or what one ought to be.

Thus, we not only have obligations to ourselves through our responsibilities to others, but we have certain immediate responsibilities to ourselves. What about the possible conflict between these two ways of being responsible to oneself? Is it possible on certain occasions for one's direct duties to oneself to be in opposition in some way with one's duties to others? Certainly situations arise in which one has to decide whether more attention should be given to obligations to others or to one's direct obligations to oneself. Such a case would be the individual who must decide whether he should work additional hours in the evening helping a friend in his business. On the one hand, he is aware that his friend has financial difficulties and that he has no one else that will help him, but he realizes that he himself is plagued with poor health and that he will endanger his life if he does not continue to get rest. This individual has a duty to help his friend, but he also has a duty to protect his health. There are other cases that concern positive benefits for oneself, but negative effects upon others. For example, a young person may recognize his personal need to develop his mental abilities through a college education, but he may also be aware of the financial burden that his education will place upon his parents. There is, therefore, a conflict between the individual's responsibility to himself and his responsibility to his parents.

In making decisions of this kind, a person must analyze the specific needs that are present to determine their importance and the probability of his being able to meet them. It is necessary for him to seek an estimation of the effect that his actions to satisfy these needs will have upon all of those involved. He must attempt to discover both the nature of this effect and the probability of its occurring. After examining the circumstances in this manner, the individual must then decide whether the needs that exist and the probability of their being met warrant the risks of the possible ill effects.

It should be noted, however, that in cases of this type one is not always obligated to make the choice that gives emphasis to one's duties to others. On some occasions, in order to be self-giving in the best possible manner, one must give favor to one's immediate duties to oneself. In the first of the two previously given examples, a situation is conceivable in which the man's ethical obligation would be to refuse to work extra hours to help his friend. The probability might be extremely high that if he did engage in any extra work he would become severely sick and even die. Under such circumstances it would be a wise and responsible act for this person not to do the work. Of course, he should seek to assist his friend in some other manner, such as loaning him money or arranging for someone else to work with him. Even if he is not able to help his friend in any way whatsoever, this does not mean that there has been an absence of self-giving in this situation. There has been a genuine act of self-giving in the sense that the individual has legitimately provided for himself.

In summary, ethical experience refers to our encounter with God that occurs through the finite universe. Out of these experiences there arise certain ethical responsibilities for man that include both duties toward others and duties toward oneself. An individual's duties toward others consist of his obligations to other human beings, to nonhuman life, and to nonliving matter, but at the same time human beings should be granted a sense of priority over that of other existents. In addition, a person's duties to himself overlap with his duties to others in the sense that by being responsible in one's relationships with others, one is also exercising self-giving toward oneself. One's duties to oneself not only demand that one be responsible toward others, but that one carry out certain immediate obligations toward oneself.

Both the mystical and ethical experiences of the Divine have now been examined. A question that arises concerns the relationship between these two kinds of experiences. What impact, if any, do they have upon each other? Do they interact with each other, and if so, in what way?

Discussion Questions

1. Does the performance of one's duties toward others always bring some sort of benefit to oneself? What does it mean to act in a selfish or self-centered manner?

2. Do you think that the following activities are ethically justified: experimentation on animals, dogfighting, cockfighting, horse racing, fishing, hunting, rodeos, and zoos? Are you aware of any practices that sometimes occur within these activities that you would consider unethical?

3. What is an anthropocentric position in regard to God's purpose in the universe? Do you think it is correct?

4. Do you think that human beings should take priority over other beings? What reasons do you have for saying that they should or should not have priority?

5. Do you think it is unethical to waste resources such as food, water, wood, paper, electricity, and gasoline? What are some examples of wasted resources in American society today?

6. Is one justified in harming or killing an animal such as a bear or a snake even if it does not pose an immediate danger to the individual?

7. Do you think there is a certain time in life in which a person should first begin developing individuation? What responsibilities do parents have in regard to the development of individuation in their children?

8. Do you agree that there are ethical obligations toward one's body? Would you point to any other particular responsibilities toward the body besides the ones mentioned within the chapter?

9. Do you think we have a responsibility to develop our mental capacity? If so, are there certain abilities that deserve special emphasis?

Suggestions for Further Reading

Abrecht, Paul, ed. *Faith, Science and the Future*. Philadelphia: Fortress Press, 1978.

Aristotle. *Nicomachean Ethics*. Indianapolis: The Bobbs-Merrill Company, Inc., 1962.

Barbour, Ian G., ed. *Earth Might Be Fair*. Englewood Cliffs NJ: Prentice-Hall, Inc., 1972.

_____, ed. *Western Man and Environmental Ethics: Attitudes Toward Nature and Technology*. Reading MA: Addison-Wesley Publishing Co., 1973.

Barnette, Henlee H. *Introducing Christian Ethics*. Nashville: Broadman Press, 1961.

Blackstone, William T., ed. *Philosophy and Environmental Crisis*. Athens GA: University of Georgia Press, 1974.

Cobb, John B. Jr. *Is It Too Late? A Theology of Ecology*. Beverly Hills CA: Benziger, Bruce and Glencoe, Inc., 1972.

Commoner, Barry. *The Poverty of Power*. New York: Bantam Books, Inc., 1976.

Fletcher, Joseph. *Situation Ethics*. Philadelphia. The Westminster Press, 1966.

Fritsch, Albert J. *Environmental Ethics*. Garden City NY: Anchor Press, 1980.

Gardner, E. Clinton. *Biblical Faith and Social Ethics*. New York: Harper and Row, 1960.

Gustafson, James M. *Ethics from a Theocentric Perspective: Theology and Ethics*. Chicago: The University of Chicago Press, 1981.

Jersild, Paul and Johnson, Dale, ed. *Moral Issues and Christian Response*. New York: Holt, Rinehart and Winston, 1971.

Kant, Immanuel. *Critique of Practical Reason*. Indianapolis: The Bobbs-Merrill Company, 1958.

_____. *Fundamental Principles of the Metaphysics of Morals*. Indianapolis: The Bobbs-Merrill Company, 1949.

_____. *Lectures on Ethics*. New York: Harper and Row, 1963.

Linzey, Andrew. *Animal Rights: A Christian Assessment of Man's Treatment of Animals*. London: SCM Press Ltd, 1976.

Regan, Tom, and Singer, Peter, ed. *Animal Rights and Human Obligations*. Englewood Cliffs NJ: Prentice-Hall, Inc., 1976.

V

The Relationship
Between the Mystical
and the Ethical

This final chapter examines the relationship between mystical and ethical experience. It points out that each of these experiences has the potential for inducing the occurrence of the other. Although there are certain factors that may interfere with this process, it is possible for the mystical to serve as a basis for the ethical and for the ethical to serve as a basis for the mystical. This chapter also investigates the nature of a fundamental analogy that exists between the mystical and the ethical. This analogy indicates that in our encounters with the Divine, the mystical and the ethical are not completely separate, but in some cases they overlap each other. In addition, this chapter demonstrates the particular implications of this relationship between the mystical and the ethical. These implications are that the Divine persuasion is working through this relationship and that the recognition of this relationship broadens one's understanding and contributes to one's communication with the Divine.

The Mystical as a Foundation
for the Ethical

In order to explore the way the mystical serves as a foundation for the ethical, it is first necessary to make reference to a previous distinction between two dimensions of the ethical. These dimensions are the reception of God's love and the extension of this love. It is possible for mystical experience to have an influence upon both of these dimensions. In regard to the ethical reception of love, mystical experience can assist an individual in becoming more aware of the Divine presence. This expanded awareness may eventually lead to a recognition of the Divine in ethical relations. In turn, this recognition may stimulate an individual to seek these ethical experiences of love more often. There is, however, an important sense in which this dimension of the ethical is independent of the mystical. As already indicated, there are numerous ways in which all persons experience Divine love through ethical relationships, and these encounters occur regardless of whether there has been a mystical experience of God. It is clear that the acceptance of love through such means as air, water, food, parental care, and friendship does not depend upon the presence of a mystical relationship.

The potential of the mystical as an influence upon the ethical is far greater in regard to its relation to the second dimension of the ethical than it is for its relation to the first dimension. It is possible for mystical experience to serve as a basis within the person for the expression of Divine love. Through a mystical encounter with the Divine, an individual gains an appreciation of Divine love, which can function as the beginning of a will to be self-giving toward the other material beings of the universe and also toward oneself. In order for this to occur, however, the individual must appropriate this love in such a way that its rightful nature is accepted. The person must understand that this love has sharing as an essential quality.

Of course, the presence of this second dimension of the ethical in a person's life does not depend upon the mystical. A willingness to express God's love does not have to come from a mystical encounter and its proper appropriation, but rather it may grow out of the ethical itself. That is, some people reach the second dimension of the ethical by means of the first dimension. They acquire the recognition of the importance of extending love to others and the will to implement these acts of sharing as a result of their experiences of love in the world. There is an acquisition of love through others and a reflection upon these experiences, and this serves as a basis for the capacity to express love in their relationships. Even in such cases as these, when this sharing capacity arises from the individual's experiences in the world, it is possible for mystical encounters to contribute to this capacity. Mystical experiences can assist in the individual's awareness of the nature of Divine love and in gaining a greater appreciation for it.

Mystical experience has the potential for stimulating an individual's ability for extending love. It can also strengthen this ethical capacity, if this dimension has already begun to develop. The results of a mystical experience, however, are not necessarily of this nature. There is no guarantee that mystical experience will have any encouraging or supportive influence upon this second dimension of the ethical. This is so because there are certain factors that are able to prevent the contribution that the mystical might make to the ethical realm. One of these factors concerns the pleasure that is derived from the mystical. As previously pointed out in chapter three, a mystical encounter produces feelings of joy and peace, which can be highly satisfying; consequently, individuals may become preoccupied with having these experiences. They may become caught up in seeking these encounters and even try to create conditions for their existence. As a result, the ethical may be delegated to an insignificant position in comparison to the emphasis given to the mystical. There may be little or no awareness or appreciation of the activity of the Divine in the ethical realm.

Another factor that is sometimes present in this regard is that of escapism. It is possible for someone who is having mystical experiences to recognize to some degree the importance of the ethical realm and the activity of the Divine within it. Yet, they may not be willing to involve themselves in it to any great extent. They may lack the concern, courage, or self-discipline required to actively participate in the sharing of love. Because of this, they may turn to an increased emphasis upon the mystical in an effort to have more of these experiences and to avoid the demands of the ethical. In this way, attention to the mystical becomes an attempt to escape from the responsibilities of the ethical.

There is still another factor that can serve to keep mystical experience from contributing to the ethical life of the individual. This factor concerns the way the individual interprets the Divine activity. Sometimes the work of the Divine in human lives is understood as coming for the most part through mystical experiences. The mystical is viewed as the only way, or at least the most prevalent and valuable way, that God reveals himself to man. Of course, the nature of a mystical experience gives itself readily to this kind of interpretation, for mystical encounters are often highly dynamic, emotional, and inspirational in character. This gives them a distinctive quality, which in turn is easily perceived as the unique or highest expression of the Divine activity. As a result, any other possible avenue for God's interaction with man may be entirely rejected or looked upon as inconsequential in comparison to the mystical.

The adoption of this approach to the mystical implies that the individual does not recognize the full scope of God's involvement with human beings. The work of God through other people and other beings is not adequately acknowledged. God is not thought of particularly as being present in the everyday objects and events of our lives. Along with this limitation upon the scope of God's activity, this interpretation also may not give sufficient attention to the sharing of God's love. Because of the emphasis that this approach gives to a direct relation to God, sharing may be defined primarily in terms of acts of devotion to God. Therefore, the responsibilities of extending this love through ethical relationships may be largely rejected.

The Ethical as a Foundation
for the Mystical

It is possible for the ethical to serve as a basis for the mystical. Of course, this does not mean that the occurrence of a mystical experience is always in some way dependent upon the ethical. The mystical occasionally arises without any particular encouragement or influence from the ethical; however, on some occasions the ethical provides a means of transition into the mystical. That is, there are instances in which the ethical assists in setting up those conditions that make a mystical experience possible. One way that this can occur is by the ethical contributing to the tolerance level of the individual. The love that comes through the ethical can provide a kind of openness toward others and to future ethical experiences. At the same time, this outlook can promote an encounter with the Divine through the mystical. It can enable the person to have the degree of receptivity to the Divine that is necessary for a mystical experience to take place.

Another way that the ethical can assist in establishing the conditions for the mystical is by encouraging the person to seek certain circumstances in life. The experience of God's love through the ethical may result in an effort to understand more thoroughly the nature of ethical experience or even perhaps to improve one's ability to extend love to others and oneself. In either case, the individual may be led to pursue self-examination as a way of increasing knowledge of the self. These acts of self-reflection may be periods that are also conducive for a mystical experience. Furthermore, ethical experience may result in a desire on the part of the individual to communicate more frequently and more closely with the Divine. In some cases, this desire may lead the individual not only toward additional ethical experiences but also toward the mystical realm. The individual may seek to enter into such acts as prayer and meditation, which would contribute especially to a mystical experience.

Just as there are factors that tend to interfere with the mystical serving as a foundation for the ethical, there are also factors that may prevent the ethical from assisting in the rise of mystical experience. One of these concerns a particular outlook on life. Life is sometimes interpreted in such a way that it does not allow for the mystical. A person may view life strictly in terms of a rational and orderly system and be closed to the possibility of anything that is unexplainable and spectacular. This does not mean that this outlook necessarily implies a neglect of the ethical. It may be accompanied by a deep appreciation for the love that is present in ethical relationships and may be heavily involved in the sharing of love. Even here, however, this approach usually demands that these events must be understood in a logical and consistent manner. Any experience that is unpredictable or mysterious is excluded from the realm of possibility.

Another factor that may interfere with the ethical serving as a foundation for the mystical is a certain life-style that a person might follow, in which one is constantly busy with everyday tasks and activities with others. The individual is so heavily involved in certain responsibilities and relationships that the mystical has little opportunity to emerge. Circumstances that help promote a mystical experience such as solitude and contemplation are seldom, if ever, included in the person's life.

Regarding the question of why this life-style arises, reference should be made to the possible motivation of genuine concern. An individual may have a strong desire to assist others and to improve society, resulting in a very busy and active life-style. Reference should also be made to possible social influences upon the person. The society in which one lives may praise and encourage this type of behavior; consequently, this way of life may become a source of increased prestige and self-esteem. Furthermore, it should also be recognized that this life-style may be grounded in a basic fear within the individual. Since there can be intense pain involved in learning about one's own weaknesses and inconsistencies, a person may be afraid to engage in any kind of self-examination. Because of this fear, the individual may utilize the life-style preoccupied with outward activity to escape any possible attention to the inward self. In order to avoid this confrontation with the self, the individual may seek to exclude certain situations from life such as solitude and quiet. Such circumstances as these not only lead to self-reflection, but often promote mystical experiences.

A third factor that may keep the ethical from leading into the mystical is concerned more with the inward condition of the individual. God reaches out to all people, but in order for the Divine to become a part of the individual, the person must be able to receive this love. Sometimes there are certain disturbing experiences that prevent the acceptance of the Divine. That is, deep involvement in experiences such as depression, guilt, or conflict with others may keep the individual from having the receptivity necessary for a mystical encounter. In situations of this kind, there may be such an intense struggle with the problem that the person is unable to be open to the possibility of the mystical.

An Analogy Between the Mystical and the Ethical

One way of viewing the relationship between the mystical and the ethical is in terms of the potential that each of these experiences has for helping produce the other. Even though there are factors that sometimes interfere, it is possible for each of these experiences to serve as a foundation for the existence of the other. Another way of viewing the relationship between these two types of experiences is in terms of a fundamental analogy that exists between the mystical and ethical realms. It is the elaboration of this analogy that provides further insights into the nature of the relationship.

One aspect of this analogy has to some degree already been indicated, but it is necessary at this point to give it specific attention. This concerns the interaction of the different expressions within each of these types of experiences. Regarding the mystical, there are, no doubt, examples of communications with the Divine in which introvertive and extrovertive experiences merge together in some fashion. For instance, it is possible for an extrovertive experience to lead into introspection and an introvertive experience. Consequently, any rigid division between these principle types of mysticism must be denied.

Likewise, there is not a sharp separation between the different expressions of the ethical. Love that is extended to others implies an extension of love to oneself, and a genuine love of oneself includes the presence of responsible acts toward others. Even one's immediate responsibilities toward oneself are connected with one's obligations to others since the proper development of these immediate responsibilities renders assistance to the fulfillment of one's duties toward others. The development of mental skills, for example, such as reading and critical thinking can provide one with new perspectives on human situations, and this in turn aids in implementing what is most beneficial for others. Furthermore, the reception of love from others is another facet of the ethical that cannot be completely isolated, for it is closely joined with the giving of love. It not only implies an agent that is involved in extending love in that particular act, but it may encourage additional acts of love. Either the agent or the recipient of the action or both may be inspired by the act toward some similar type of deed.

The mystical and the ethical are alike with each containing elements that adjoin or overlap in some way. The other aspect of this analogy between the mystical and the ethical concerns the close relationship between the principal types of mysticism and certain forms of ethical experience. One of these is the similar nature of introvertive mysticism and the immediate ethical relationships with oneself. It is true that introvertive mysticism is concerned exclusively with the inward self and the experiences that arise from it, whereas the ethical responsibilities towards oneself give consideration to all phases of the self including the physical and the social. Nevertheless, there are ethical duties to oneself such as individuation and the development of one's mental capacity that do have reference to one's inward self. What is the relationship between these responsibilities and introvertive mysticism? They are alike since both give attention to the inner self, but in introvertive mysticism this attention serves to bring about the mystical intuition. Introspection is not in itself the experience of the Divine, but it provides the means that enables the experience to occur. In the ethical encounters with oneself that involve the inward self, the communication with the Divine comes through the

relationship with oneself. Love is given and received in the inward interaction with oneself.

In addition, there is a similarity between extrovertive encounters and
those ethical relationships that are involved with others. Both extrovertive mysticism and ethical relations with others include the perception of
physical objects. There is a difference, however, in the part that the objects play in the experiences. In an extrovertive encounter the interaction
with these objects takes on a secondary significance. The perceptions do
serve to instigate the mystical intuition, but they are not at the center of
the experience. The essence of the experience is the direct intuition of the
Divine that results from these perceptions. In contrast, in an ethical encounter with another the focus of attention is the association with the
other physical being. The relationship with the other being serves as the
location of the experience with the Divine. God's love is received and extended in this relationship itself and not apart from it.

There is, therefore, a resemblance between these mystical and ethical
encounters, but there is a difference between them that should be noted.
This difference concerns whether the objects themselves provide the experience of the Divine or whether the objects merely provide a means by
which an intuition of the Divine occurs. Certainly this cannot be said to
be a rigid distinction between these two types of experiences. It is possible
and is probably often the case that extrovertive experiences are accompanied by ethical experiences. That is, the perceptions that give rise to
extrovertive experiences may in themselves be ethical encounters with
the Divine. Furthermore, introvertive intuitions and certain ethical experiences may also overlap with each other in that the acts of introspection may be ethical encounters.

These previous references to Divine encounters are ones in which the
mystical and the ethical experiences are interconnected, and in such cases
the mystical and the ethical are still to some degree separate and distin-
guishable. There are also encounters that participate in both categories at
the same time. In other words, there is not always a temporal differentia-
tion between the mystical and ethical elements during an encounter. The
Divine may be simultaneously experienced through objects and in a directly intuitive manner. In fact, every intuitive grasp of the Divine is always accompanied by the presence of God's love through objects if
reference is made to a necessary element such as oxygen. There are additional cases, however, in which love is at the same time acquired

through people or other life forms and in some mystical manner. Even if the love received through the object occurs first and in some way serves to encourage the intuition, the two may at some point exist together.

An individual, therefore, may have mystical and ethical experiences that overlap with each other, but it is also the case that the Divine experiences of one individual may in some way be joined with the Divine experiences of another. The ethical experience of one person may inspire another individual toward a mystical experience, and one person's mystical experience may encourage others to engage in ethical encounters. In addition, these ethical and mystical experiences, which are interconnected between different persons, may not always be temporally detached from each other, but instead may at some point exist at the same time. This means that the experiences by which mankind as a whole has contact with the Divine must be viewed as a continuum. That is, the Divine encounters of various people merge and interlink to form a continuous flow of experiences.

Thus, within human experience the mystical and the ethical are not sharply separated categories. This does not mean that a distinction between the mystical and the ethical should not be drawn, for such a distinction can be valuable in understanding our relationship to God. It does imply that this distinction is not absolute and that any use of it should be made with this recognition.

The Meaning of the Relationship

An explanation has now been given for the way the mystical and the ethical are related to each other. It has been demonstrated that each of these experiences is capable of serving as a foundation for the existence of the other and that the mystical and the ethical are to some extent intertwined. Still the specific meaning of this relationship must be examined. What are the implications of the mystical and the ethical being related in this manner? What exactly does this relationship mean for our understanding of God and our encounter with him?

One of the implications of this relationship is its suggestion that the Divine persuasion works through this process. It was pointed out in chapter two that God operates through all of the circumstances that confront a person, including the interaction of certain factors such as feelings, thoughts, and events as well as the individual expression of these various factors. It is now apparent that God is active in the interrelationship of the mystical and ethical encounters of a person's life. If God is concerned with the entire human situation and is seeking to encourage each individual toward what he wants him to be, he obviously is active in this interrelationship. That is, God is involved in those occurrences in which the mystical and the ethical influence each other or are interconnected in some way.

The life of Saint Augustine, as previously stated, was an illustration of the activity of the Divine persuasion. His life is an example of the operation of the Divine persuasion through the relationship of the mystical and the ethical. There is a sense in which the mystical is a foundation for the ethical in Augustine's life. Augustine's mystical encounter with God in his garden gave rise to numerous ethical experiences of the Divine in his life. For one thing, it started him on his way to a greater extension of love to others through his ministry as a priest. In another regard, this experience no doubt helped him to have a greater degree of self-love. It encouraged him toward the need for self-control, thereby enhancing his respect for himself. Moreover, this mystical encounter seemed to contribute to an expanded awareness of the love that comes from others. For instance, his mother had intensely hoped and prayed that Augustine would eventually accept Christianity. After his mystical encounter, Augustine appears to have an increased appreciation for her efforts and concern for him.[1]

For Augustine's life there is a sense in which the ethical served as a foundation for the mystical. His contact with different reading material, including Scripture, and his association with Christians obviously provided a basis for his mystical encounter. They led him to examine himself and to question his accepted views and life-style. At the same time, they stimulated him toward a greater degree of openness to new ideas and to the possibility of a new relationship with the Divine.[2]

Augustine's life, therefore, demonstrates that the Divine persuasion also works through the relationship of mystical and ethical experiences in a person's life. But the Divine persuasion does not simply work through

---

[1]Aurelius Augustine, *The Confessions of Saint Augustine* (New York: Pocket Books, Inc., 1951) 147-301; Frederick Copleston, *A History of Philosophy* (Garden City NY: Doubleday and Company, Inc., 1962) 2:59-62.

[2]Augustine, 104-47; Copleston, 57-58.

the interaction of these experiences in the lives of individuals. God also operates through their interaction in mankind as a whole. As already indicated, people have encounters with God that influence and overlap with the Divine experiences of others. In this way there is a continuum of experiences by which mankind encounters the Divine. Since God is interested in the welfare of all humanity, he is active in this continuum seeking to improve both mankind as a whole and each particular person.

One aspect of the meaning of the relationship between the mystical and the ethical is that God is involved in the interaction between these two types of experience. Another aspect of this meaning concerns our recognition of this relationship. An awareness of both this relationship and the work of the Divine persuasion provides an individual with a broader and richer understanding of God, the human condition, and man's relationship to God. The individual is able to avoid thinking in terms of God's love and activity as being confined to only one form or a few types of relationships. Instead, there is the understanding that God works in many different ways. He operates not only through a variety of human activities and a large number of divergent kinds of beings, but through the process by which these experiences develop and join together. At the same time, there is the rejection of a segmented view of one's relationship to the Divine. When there is this broad understanding of God's involvement with man, the individual does not tend to consider his relationship with God as only occurring at particular times and places or merely through certain beings. The person thinks of his relationship with the Divine more in terms of its being a continuous process.

Furthermore, this means that this awareness has the potential for deepening one's personal relationship with the Divine and increasing one's enjoyment of life. If one accepts that God operates in numerous ways and that one's relationship with him is a continuous experience, this can produce a much greater appreciation for the Divine and for life itself. In turn, this can bring about the desire to have a closer communion with him and to assist in the Divine activity in the universe. This acceptance also can expand one's receptivity to the Divine. When the individual's understanding of God's involvement with man is enlarged, a greater openness to God's activity results. The person can become more alert to Divine acts of love and better able to fully experience them.

In summary, one perspective on the relationship between the mystical and the ethical points to the potential that each of these areas has for helping produce the other, even though there are factors that may prevent this process from taking place. Another perspective on this relationship reveals an analogy that exists between these two realms of experience. An examination of this analogy demonstrates that the mystical and the ethical are not completely independent areas, but that they interact with each other in various ways. Moreover, the implied meaning of these perspectives is that the Divine is involved in the relationship between the mystical and the ethical and that an awareness of this relationship can enhance one's experiences of the Divine.

Discussion Questions

1. Are you aware of any religious groups or activities today that you would say are preoccupied with seeking pleasurable experiences? Are there any dangers in this kind of approach?

2. What is the nature of escapism as it is presented in this chapter? Do you think this is a serious problem today in the sense of preventing people from carrying out ethical responsibilities?

3. To what extent does God work through other means besides mystical experiences? Do you think we should give more attention to emphasizing these other forms of Divine activity?

4. How prevalent in our society is the outlook that stresses a logical and explainable world order and that has difficulty accepting that which is unpredictable and unusual? What elements in our society might influence people toward the adoption of this viewpoint?

5. What are the reasons given in this chapter for a person accepting a highly active and busy life-style? Are there any other reasons that you would give for why people are involved in this way of life?

6. What are the different aspects of the analogy between the mystical and the ethical that are set forth in this chapter? What does this analogy reveal about the way the Divine is experienced?

7. What is meant when it is said in this chapter that mankind's experiences of the Divine form a continuum? Is it correct to say that each individual's encounters with God also form a continuum?

8. What examples would you give for the activity of the Divine persuasion in the relationship of the mystical and the ethical?

9. What is meant by a segmented view of one's relationship to God? Do you think it is common in our society for people to understand their relationship to God in this way?

Suggestions for Further Reading

Berdyaev, Nicholas. *The Destiny of Man*. New York: Harper and Row, 1960.

Bergson, Henri. *The Two Sources of Morality and Religion*. New York: Henry Holt and Company, 1935.

Bonhoeffer, Dietrich. *Letters and Papers from Prison*. New York: Macmillan Publishing Co., Inc., 1953.

Edwards, Rem B. *Reason and Religion: An Introduction to the Philosophy of Religion*. New York: Harcourt Brace Jovanovich, 1972.

Kant, Immanuel. *Religion Within the Limits of Reason Alone*. New York: Harper and Row, 1960.

Keen, Sam. *Apology For Wonder*. New York: Harper and Row, 1969.

_____. *To A Dancing God*. New York: Harper and Row, 1970.

Kierkegaard, Søren. *Concluding Unscientific Postscript*. Princeton: Princeton University Press, 1941.

_____. *Fear and Trembling*. Princeton: Princeton University Press, 1941.

Outka, Gene, and Reeder, John, P., eds. *Religion and Morality: A Collection of Essays*. Garden City NY: Anchor Press, 1973.

Taylor, Richard. *With Heart and Mind*. New York: St. Martin's Press, 1973.

Tillich, Paul. *Dynamics of Faith*. New York: Harper and Row, 1957.

Bibliography

Augustine, Aurelius. *The Confessions of Saint Augustine*. New York: Pocket Books, Inc., 1951.

Cobb, John B. *A Christian Natural Theology*. Philadelphia: The Westminster Press, 1965.

Copleston, Frederick. *A History of Philosophy*. Garden City NY: Doubleday and Company, Inc., vol. 2, part 1, 1962.

Gustafson, James M. *Ethics from a Theocentric Perspective: Theology and Ethics*. Chicago: The University of Chicago Press, 1981.

Happold, F. C. *Mysticism: A Study and an Anthology*. Baltimore: Penguin Books, 1963.

Harkness, Georgia. *Mysticism, Its Meaning and Message*. Nashville: Abingdon Press, 1973.

Jersild, Paul and Johnson, Dale, eds. *Moral Issues and Christian Response*. New York: Holt, Rinehart and Winston, 1971.

Kant, Immanuel. *Lectures on Ethics*. New York: Harper and Row, 1963.

Kierkegaard, Søren. *Either/Or*. Garden City NY: Doubleday and Company, 1959.

_____. *Works of Love*. New York: Harper and Row, 1962.

May, Rollo. *The Art of Counseling*. Nashville: Abingdon Press, 1939.

_____. *Love and Will*. New York: Dell Publishing Co., 1969.

Nietzsche, Friedrich. *Human, All-Too-Human*, part 1. New York: Russell and Russell, Inc., 1964.

Otto, Rudolf. *Mysticism, East and West*. New York: Macmillan Publishing Co., 1932.

Regan, Tom, and Singer, Peter, eds. *Animal Rights and Human Obligations*. Englewood Cliffs NJ: Prentice-Hall, Inc., 1976.

Sartre, Jean-Paul. *Being and Nothingness*. New York: Washington Press, Inc., 1953.

Schleiermacher, Friedrich. *On Religion: Speeches to Its Cultured Despisers*. New York: Harper and Row, 1958.

Stace, Walter T. *The Teachings of the Mystics*. New York: New American Library, 1960.

Tillich, Paul. *The Shaking of the Foundations*. New York: Charles Scribner's Sons, 1948.

_____. *Systematic Theology*. Volume 2. Chicago: The University of Chicago Press, 1957.

Index

MUP *Mystical and Ethical Experience*
Designed by Alesa Jones
Composition by MUP Composition Department
Production specifications:
    text paper—60-lb. Warren's Olde Style
    endpapers—Multicolor Antique Dove Grey
    covers—(on .088 boards) Holliston Roxite B
        51567 Vellum
    dust jacket—100-lb. enamel printed two
        colors, PMS 175 (brown) and PMS 468 (beige) and varnished
Printing (offset lithography) and binding by
    OMNIPRESS of Macon, Inc., Macon, Georgia